N

LO

TOURIST

ATLAS & GUIDE

1 **LONDON GUIDE**

Getting About *3*; Free Entertainment *4*; Sightseeing *5*; Museums and Galleries *6*; Outdoor London *7*; Taking to the River *8*; Cultural Entertainment *8*; Live Music *10*; Activities *11*; Sinister London *12*; Shopping *12*; Markets *14*; Eating and Drinking *14*.

2 **CENTRAL LONDON**

Large scale maps showing the areas adjacent to Piccadilly Circus, *18*; Theatres & cinemas map, *26*.

3 **LONDON**

Key map, *28*; Detailed maps covering inner London between Regent's Park and the Oval and from Kensington to the London Docks, *30*; Underground map, *64*; Shopping map, *66*; Late and All-night London, *67*; Helpful Information, *69*.

4 **STREET INDEX**

Over 4,000 street names from both map sections are listed in the index, *71*.

Map references
The letters A or B precede the map page number and indicate
whether the street is to be found in the upper half of the page (A),
or (B) the lower half.

First published 1990

© **Nicholson 1990**

Nicholson is an imprint of
Bartholomew, A Division of
HarperCollins Publishers

Central London and London Maps
© **Nicholson 1990**
based upon the Ordnance Survey with the sanction of the
controller of Her Majesty's Stationery Office.
Crown Copyright reserved.

London Underground map by
kind permission of London Regional Transport.
Registered User Number 90/067

All other maps
© Nicholson

Nicholson
16 Golden Square
London W1R 4BN

Great care has been taken throughout this book to be accurate,
but the publishers cannot accept responsibility for any errors
which appear or their consequences.

Typeset by Rowland Phototypesetting Limited
Bury St Edmunds, Suffolk
Printed by Bartholomew in Edinburgh, Scotland

C/J3892   END
90/1/135

London Guide

GETTING ABOUT

TOURIST INFORMATION
British Travel Centre   **A22**
Rex House, 4–12 Lower Regent St SW1. 071-730 3400. British
Tourist Authority, American Express Travel Service Office, British
Rail ticket office and a bureau de change. Also booking services for
theatre tickets, hotel rooms, car hire, air and coach travel. Book shop,
gift shop and regular exhibitions. *Open 09.00–18.30 Mon–Fri, 09.00
–17.00 Sat, 10.00–16.00 Sun.*.

City of London Information Centre   **B43**
St Paul's Churchyard EC4. 071-606 3030. All about the City. Monthly
Diary of Events which lists free entertainments.

London Tourist Board Information Centre   **A59**
Victoria Station Forecourt SW1. Multi-lingual tourist and travel in-
formation for London and Britain. Also instant hotel reservations,
theatre and tour bookings. Bookshop. *Open 08.00–20.00 Mon–Sun
Easter–Oct; 09.00–19.00 Mon–Sat, 09.00–17.00 Sun Oct–Easter.*
Telephone information service: 071-730 3488.

Harrods, Knightsbridge SW1   **B48**
Heathrow Central Underground Station
Selfridges, 400 Oxford St W1   **B38**
Tower of London, West Gate E1   **A55**
Liverpool Street Station   **B44**

TRAVEL
Buses and underground trains usually run between *05.30 and 24.00*.
However, there is also a night bus network serving all major points in
Central London. London Transport offers a free *24hr* Travel Informa-
tion Service on 071-222 1234. All underground stations have a notice
of first and last trains. Some bus stops list first and last buses.

London Transport Travel Information Centres
For enquiries on tube and bus travel, sightseeing tours and special
cut-price touring tickets:
Euston Underground Station   **B33**
Heathrow Central Underground Station
King's Cross Underground Station   **A34**
Oxford Circus Underground Station   **B40**
Piccadilly Circus Underground Station   **A50**
Victoria Underground Station   **A59**

FREE ENTERTAINMENT

How to spend a pleasant hour or so without spending money. Here are some famous London attractions.

CHANGING OF THE GUARD
Telephone London Tourist Board (071-730 3488) for details.

Buckingham Palace   **B49**
SW1. New guard marches from Chelsea or Wellington Barracks; changes *11.30 daily, alt days in winter.*

Horseguards Parade   **B51**
Whitehall SW1. Queen's Life Guard, on great black horses, leave Hyde Park Barracks *10.38 Mon–Sat, 09.39 Sun.* Ceremony *11.00 Mon–Sat, 10.00 Sun.*

CHURCH CONCERTS
Free lunchtime concerts, though there is usually a collection.

St Bride   **B42**
Fleet St EC4. 071-353 1301. *13.15 Tue, Wed & Fri.*

St John's   **A61**
Smith Sq SW1. 071-222 1061. *13.00 Mon & 13.15 alt Thur.*

St Martin-in-the-Fields   **A51**
Trafalgar Sq WC2. 071-839 1930. *13.05 Mon, Tue & Fri.*

HOUSES OF PARLIAMENT   **A61**
St Margaret St SW1. 071-219 3000. Look around the Victorian-Gothic pile (built 1840–68 by Sir Charles Barry and A. W. N. Pugin) when Parliament is in recess. *Jul/Aug–Oct.* (Permission from your MP or through your embassy is necessary.) Or queue for admission during debates. Be sure to admire the famous clock, 'Big Ben'.

MILITARY AND BRASS BANDS
For rousing British music try one of these parks on a summer afternoon. Check *What's On* and *Time Out* for details.

Hyde Park   **B46**
W1. *Every afternoon and early eve Mon–Sun.*

Regent's Park   **A32**
NW1. *Every lunchtime and early eve Mon–Fri, Sun & B. hols.*

St James's Park   **B50**
SW1. *Every lunchtime and early eve Mon–Fri, Sun & B. hols.*

OLD BAILEY   **B43**
Old Bailey EC4. 071-248 3277. Central criminal court. Trials open to the public. Minimum age 14. *Mon–Fri.*

SPEAKER'S CORNER   **A48**
Marble Arch corner of Hyde Park. Where unknown orators explain their views of life. Feel free to argue. *Sun.*

SIGHTSEEING

Buckingham Palace   B49
St James's Park SW1. London residence of the Sovereign (the Royal Standard flies when the Queen is at home). Built 1705, remodelled by Nash, 1825, refaced by Sir Ashton Webb 1913.

The Cenotaph   B51
Whitehall SW1. Designed 1920 by Sir Edward Lutyens to honour the dead of World War I. Wreaths are laid here annually at the culmination of the Remembrance Day Service in memory of those who fell in both world wars.

City of London   B44
The 'square mile' of the City is the oldest part of London and the centre of banking, insurance and stockbroking. Look for sections of the Roman Wall, medieval streets and alleys, old taverns and churches that survived the Great Fire of 1666.

Covent Garden   B41
The former home of the famous fruit and vegetable market—today one of London's most popular meeting places. Grand Victorian warehouses shelter craft shops, gift stalls, wine bars, restaurants and art galleries. Originally designed by Inigo Jones in the 1630s.

Downing Street   B51
17thC houses built by Sir George Downing. No 10 is the official residence of the Prime Minister, No 11 of the Chancellor of the Exchequer. Handy for the Houses of Parliament, the offices and Ministries of Whitehall.

Fleet Street   B42
The street of communications and the law. Few national newspapers still have their offices on or near it, many having moved eastwards to the Docklands redevelopment area.

Piccadilly Circus   B40
Six major streets converge at the fountain and statue of Eros (Gilbert 1892). No longer glamorous but its fame lingers on.

St Paul's Cathedral   B43
Ludgate Hill EC4. 071-248 4619/2705. Built by Christopher Wren from 1675–1710, and considered his greatest work. Superb dome, porches and monuments. The setting in 1981 for the marriage of Charles, Prince of Wales and Lady Diana Spencer.

Soho   B40
London's oldest 'foreign quarter', encompassing the whole of Chinatown. Plenty of restaurants, foreign food shops and pubs. Soho's sleazy image is gradually disappearing and the area is becoming the trendy place for designer clothes and fashionable bars and cafés.

The Temple   A52
Inner Temple, Crown Office Row EC4. 071-353 8462. Middle Temple, Middle Temple Lane EC4. 071-353 4355. Two Inns of Court. Wander round the courtyards, alleys, gardens and the early Gothic 'round' church built by the Templars. *Open 10.00–16.00 Mon–Fri.*

Tower Bridge   **B55**
Twin Victorian-Gothic towers with a hydraulic drawbridge, 1894.
Breathtaking views from the high walkways. Museum on south side
displays the Victorian steam engines that powered it.

Trafalgar Square   **A51**
Nelson's column (1840) guarded by Landseer's bronze lions. Meeting place for political demonstrators and pigeons.

Westminster Abbey   **A61**
(The Collegiate Church of St Peter in Westminster) Broad Sanctuary
SW1. 071-222 5152. Original church by Edward the Confessor,
1065. Rebuilt by Henry III from 1245 and completed 1376–1506.
Fine perpendicular with fan vaulting. Contains Coronation Chair,
tombs and memorials of the Royalty of England.

MUSEUMS AND GALLERIES

British Museum   **A41**
Great Russell St WC1. 071-636 1555. One of the largest and greatest
in the world – Egyptian mummies, Assyrian bulls, Elgin Marbles,
Rosetta Stone. *Closed Sun morn.*

Hayward Gallery   **B52**
Belvedere Rd SE1. 071-928 3144. Riverside gallery hosting major art
exhibitions. *Admission charge.*

Imperial War Museum   **A62**
Lambeth Rd SE1. 071-416 5000. National collection concerned with
all aspects of war since 1914, contained in an ex-lunatic asylum.

Madame Tussauds   **A38**
Marylebone Rd NW1. 071-935 6861. Waxen images of the famous
and notorious, life-size and life-like. Chamber of Horrors gets the
adrenalin going. *Admission charge.*

Museum of London   **A43**
London Wall EC2. 071-600 3699. A 3-dimensional history of the City
and London area. *Closed Sun morn and Mon.*

National Gallery   **A51**
Trafalgar Sq WC2. 071-839 3321. Built 1838 by W. Wilkins and
containing a fine representative collection of the various schools of
painting. *Closed Sun morn.*

Natural History Museum   **A57**
Cromwell Rd SW7. 071-589 6323. Exhibitions of zoology, ento-
mology, palaeontology and botany. *Closed Sun morn. Admission
charge.*

Planetarium   **A38**
Marylebone Rd NW1. 071-486 1121. Beginner's guide to the galaxy.
The universe is represented hourly on the domed ceiling, with a
commentary. *Admission charge.*

Science Museum   **A57**
Exhibition Rd SW7. 071-589 3456. Large collection of working

models and special exhibitions on the history of science and its application to industry.

Tate Gallery   **B61**
Millbank SW1. 071-821 1313. Famous for its representative collections of British paintings from the 16thC to the present day; also rich in foreign paintings and British and European sculpture. *Closed Sun morn.*

Victoria & Albert Museum   **A57**
Cromwell Rd SW7. 071-589 6371. Vast collection of decorative art from all categories, countries and ages. Over 10 acres of museum. *Closed Sun morn.*

Wallace Collection   **B38**
Hertford House, Manchester Sq W1. 071-935 0687. Fine private collection of paintings, furniture, porcelain and armour, bequeathed to the nation by Lady Wallace in 1897. *Closed Sun morn.*

OUTDOOR LONDON

Hampstead Heath, NW3
081-340 5603. 790 acres of parkland, sandy hills and wooded valleys. Once haunted by highwaymen, now crowded with visitors to the Bank Holiday fairs and famous inns – The Bull & Bush, Spaniard's Inn and Jack Straw's Castle. Superb views. Also, wander through the streets of Hampstead – famous for its literary and artistic connections, as well as its appealing 'village' atmosphere.

Hyde Park, W1   **A47**
071-262 5484. 340 acres of Royal parkland with Rotten Row for horse riders, the Serpentine lake for fishing, boating, swimming and admiring the ducks. There's also an open-air bar and restaurant for the hungry and thirsty.

Jason's Trip
Opp 60 Blomfield Rd W9. 071-286 3428. Traditional narrow boats make 1½ hr return trips through Regent's Park and Zoo to Camden Lock.

Kensington Gardens, W8   **A46**
071-937 4848. An elegant addition to Hyde Park, containing Kensington Palace, the peaceful sunken garden, Round Pond, Albert Memorial – and Peter Pan's statue.

Kenwood House
Hampstead Lane NW3. 081-348 1286. 18thC Robert Adam house, with fine art collection and superb grounds. On Sat in summer, leading orchestras give lakeside concerts. Take a picnic. Book for tickets on 071-379 4444.

The London Zoo   **A32**
Regent's Park NW1. 071-722 3333. By Decimus Burton, 1827. Since then, famous architects have designed new quarters for one of the largest animal collections in the world. First class children's zoo. *Admission charge.*

Regent's Park Open Air Theatre **B31**
Inner Circle, Regent's Park NW1. 071-486 2431. Round off a fine day
by watching a play, usually Shakespearean, in an attractive outdoor
setting. *May–Sept.*

St James's Park SW1 **B50**
071-262 5484. The oldest Royal park with a Chinese-style lake,
bridge and weeping willows. Richly populated bird sanctuary on
Duck Island presided over by the pelicans.

TAKING TO THE RIVER

Good way to see London when the weather is fine. You can
telephone the special River Boat Information Service on 071-730
4812. Below are two of the best trips.

GREENWICH
Westminster Pier **B51**
Victoria Embankment SW1. 071-930 4097. Boats leave for Green-
wich about *every 30 mins.*

The 'Cutty Sark'
King William Wlk SE10. 081-858 3445. Visit one of the great sailing
tea clippers. *Closed Sun morn. Admission charge.*

National Maritime Museum
Romney Rd SE10. 081-858 4422. Finest maritime collection in
Britain. Incorporates Queen's House by Inigo Jones, 1616, and the
Old Royal Observatory with its astronomical instruments and
Planetarium. *Closed Sun morn.*

Royal Naval College
Greenwich SE10. 081-858 2154. Fine group of classical buildings by
Webb, Wren and Vanbrugh, fronting on to the river. Chapel by James
Stuart, Painted Hall by Thornhill. *Closed morn & Thur.*

KEW
Boats leave Westminster Pier for Kew *about every 30 mins.*

Royal Botanic Gardens
Kew Rd, Surrey. 081-940 1171. One of the world's great botanic
gardens with magnificent Victorian planthouses. 300 acres of green
peace and unusual flowers. *Small charge.*

CULTURAL ENTERTAINMENT

For music, opera, ballet or theatre it is wise to book seats in advance
at the Box Office (a Ticket Agency will charge commission). If you
can face possible disappointment, try for 'returns' just before the
performance. Brief details and times appear in *Time Out, The
Evening Standard*, and the national newspapers.

MUSIC

Royal Albert Hall   B46
Kensington Gore SW7. 071-589 8212. Huge, Victorian domed hall famous for the 'Proms'. Mainly orchestral and choral, but also pop concerts, sporting events and meetings.

Royal Festival Hall   A52
South Bank SE1. 071-928 8800. Built 1951 as part of South Bank Arts Centre. Orchestral and choral concerts here, or in adjacent Queen Elizabeth Hall and Purcell Room.

St John's   A61
Smith Sq SW1. 071-222 1061. Solo recitals, chamber, orchestral and choral works in a unique 18thC church. Restaurant and art exhibitions in the crypt.

Wigmore Hall   B39
36 Wigmore St W1. 071-935 2141. By tradition, visiting musicians make their London debut in its intimate atmosphere. Chiefly chamber music and solo recitals.

OPERA AND BALLET

Coliseum   A51
St Martin's Lane WC2. 071-836 3161. Opera in English from the English National Opera (and visiting companies). Also ballet performed for audiences of up to 2,400.

Royal Opera House, Covent Garden   B41
Bow St WC2. 071-240 1066. 24hr information on 0898-600 001. Where to see the world-famous Royal Opera and Royal Ballet companies. Those in the expensive seats often dress up for the occasion.

Sadler's Wells   B35
Rosebery Av EC1. 071-278 8916. The original well discovered by Thomas Sadler is under a trap-door at the back of the stalls. Birthplace of the Royal Ballet Company; now used by visiting opera and dance companies.

THEATRE

London has had live theatre for seven centuries. Today the greatest concentration of theatres is along, or just off, Shaftesbury Avenue, Leicester Square and within the Covent Garden area. See 'Theatres & Cinemas Map' on page 26.

Barbican (RSC)   A43
Barbican Centre, Barbican EC2. 071-628 3351. Purpose-built for the Royal Shakespeare Company. A large theatre for large scale productions and The Pit for the performance of work by new British playwrights. See Shakespeare, revivals and classics.

Comedy   A50
Panton St SW1. 071-867 1045. Good intimate theatre showing unusual comedy and small cast plays.

Haymarket (Theatre Royal)   A50
Haymarket SW1. 071-930 9832. Originally built in 1720 as 'The Little

Theatre in the Hay'. Present theatre was designed by Nash in 1821. Stages quality plays.

Lyric **B40**
Shaftesbury Av W1. 071-437 3686. Oldest theatre in Shaftesbury Avenue, built in 1888. Sarah Bernhardt performed here. Today, mainly plays and musicals.

National Theatre **A52**
South Bank SE1. 071-928 2252. The large apron-staged Olivier, smaller Lyttelton, and adaptable Cottesloe are the home of the National Theatre Company and stage a wide variety of plays. Daytime tours take you backstage and into the workshops.

Palladium **B40**
8 Argyll St W1. 071-437 7373. Houses top variety shows, the annual Royal Command Performance and a pantomime at Christmas.

Vaudeville **A51**
Strand WC2. 071-836 9988. Listed building. Originally ran farce and burlesque, then became straight. Now a mixture of the two.

LIVE MUSIC

For live music in a relaxed setting you can't beat the pubs and clubs. The charge is rarely high and membership, if necessary, is usually available at the door. For details see *Time Out* or the music press.

Bass Clef
35 Coronet St, off Hoxton Sq N1. 071-729 2476. A very popular basement venue hosting jazz, Latin American and African bands. *Admission charge.*

Bull's Head
373 Lonsdale Rd, Barnes SW13. 071-876 5241. Worth the trip south of the river to hear good modern jazz, every evening and Sun lunchtime, from top English and visiting foreign players.

Dover Street Wine Bar **A49**
8–9 Dover St W1. 071-629 9813. Different bands every night – predominantly jazz but also some blues and soul.

Half Moon
93 Lower Richmond Rd, Putney SW15. 081-788 2387. To the south again for this large pub with its spacious back room where live music is played every night and on Sun lunchtime. Jazz, folk, rock, R & B and soul.

100 Club **A20**
100 Oxford St W1. 071-636 0933. Friendly and comfortable jazz club featuring live bands (trad, modern, African). Two bars.

Prospect of Whitby
57 Wapping Wall E1. 071-481 1095. Once used by so many thieves and smugglers they called it 'The Devil's Tavern'. Live music on *Thur, Fri & Sun* ranging from South American to jazz and R&B. Restaurant with terrace overlooks the river.

Rock Garden **B41**
6–7 The Piazza, Covent Garden WC2. 071-240 3961. American-style restaurant upstairs and on street level. Downstairs, two bands nightly. Blues, rock, indie and house.
Ronnie Scott's **B40**
46–49 Frith St W1. 071-439 0747. Enjoy the best jazz in London in a comfortable atmosphere with subtle lighting and good food. *Closed Sun. Admission charge.*
Torrington
4 Lodge Lane N12. 081-445 4710. Well-known in the pub circuit for some top names in jazz rock. Resident and visiting bands play in the restaurant. *Fri & Sun nights.*

ACTIVITIES

If the mixture of culture and night life is wearing you out, a bit of healthy exercise could work wonders.

SKATING
Pay by the session and for skate hire. Tuition an optional extra.
Picketts Lock Centre
Picketts Lock Lane N9. 081-803 4756. Indoor roller skating rink. *Mon only.*
Queen's Ice Skating Club **B36**
17 Queensway W2. 071-229 0172. If your wheels are running away with you, change to blades and cut a dash on the ice. Crowded and sociable with a licensed bar to help restore lost confidence.

SPORTS CENTRES
Well equipped with wide ranging classes and facilities, if you want to use the more popular facilities it is wise to book in advance.
Crystal Palace National Sports Centre
Crystal Palace SE19. 081-778 0131. Largest multi-sports centre in the country, right in Crystal Palace Park. Facilities include dry-skiing, squash, tennis, swimming. Fully equipped indoor sports hall. *Day membership scheme. Open to 22.00.*
Jubilee Hall **B21**
Covent Garden Piazza WC2. 071-836 4835. Centrally placed sports centre with large multi-gym and wide range of classes.
YMCA: London Central **A41**
112 Great Russell St WC1. 071-637 8131. Welcomes local and overseas members of both sexes. Indoor only, including gymnastics, weight-training, aerobics, swimming, table tennis and yoga. *Membership necessary.*

WALKING TOURS
A guided walk, usually with a special theme, is an inexpensive way of seeing more of London.

London Walks
22 Kingdon Rd NW6. 071-435 6413. Meet at various tube stations for walks (1½–2hrs) with titles like Legal and Illegal London, An Historic Pub Walk and The Famous Square Mile. *Mon–Sun all year round.*
Streets of London
16 The Grove N3. 081-346 9225. Walks offered include The London of Jack the Ripper, Sherlock Holmes and Haunted London. Phone for details.

SINISTER LONDON

The older parts of London are somewhat grisly anyway, with their history of murder, martyrdom and ghosts. But if you relish the gruesome, try these extras.
Discovering London
11 Pennyfield, Worley, Brentwood, Essex. Brentwood 213704. Shuddery organised walks including Ghosts and Pubs, Night Prowl.
Highgate Cemetery
Swains Lane N6. 081-340 1834. Most graveyards have a certain creepy splendour – this one also has the dust of the famous, including Karl Marx, George Eliot and Michael Faraday.

London Dungeon   **B54**
28–34 Tooley St SE1. 071-403 0606. A horror museum in suitably unpleasant surroundings – huge damp vaults under London Bridge Station. Scenes of medieval torture garnished with stage blood. *Admission charge.*

Tower of London   **A55**
Tower Hill EC3. 071-709 0765. Grim and famous fortress guarded by Beefeaters and ravens. See Traitors Gate (entrance of the doomed), armoury, executioner's block and axe and the Crown Jewels. *Admission charge.*

Town of Ramsgate   **A55**
62 Wapping High St E1. 071-488 2685. At the end of an eerie day, restore the nerves with a drink in this 17thC riverside tavern, where, nearby, Colonel Blood was caught while trying to escape with the Crown Jewels. And below, evil Judge Jeffries watched as pirates and smugglers were tied up and drowned by the incoming tide.

SHOPPING

London is immensely rich in shops, from large department stores to small specialists. The four main West End shopping streets are: the very crowded Oxford Street for department stores, clothes and shoes; the more sedate Regent Street for expensive clothes, china

and glass; Tottenham Court Road for electronics and furniture; and Bond Street for luxurious clothes, rugs, jewellery and pictures. *Most shops open 09.00–17.30 Mon–Sat.* Try:

Anything Left Handed A50

65 Beak St W1. 071-437 3910. For the south-paws back home. More than 100 left-handed gadgets always in stock. *Closed Sat afternoons.*

Covent Garden General Store B41

111 Long Acre WC2. 071-240 0331. A large and bright store overflowing with gifts and novelties to solve every present problem. Basketware, bags, scarves, cosmetics, stationery and lots of gimmicky gift ideas. *Open 09.00–24.00 Mon–Sat, 11.00–19.00 Sun.*

The Design Centre A50

28 Haymarket SW1. 071-839 8000. Large showroom of the best in British design. Excellent shop and bookshop.

Fortnum & Mason A50

181 Piccadilly W1. 071-734 8040. Elegant store selling luscious selection of foods from all over the world. Also china and glassware. Expensive, beautiful designer clothes.

Foyles B40

119–125 Charing Cross Rd WC2. 071-437 5660. The biggest of the bookshops. Aims to stock virtually every British book currently in print.

Habitat A40

196 Tottenham Court Rd W1. 071-631 3880. A member of Sir Terence Conran's hugely successful furniture and household goods chain. Good design at affordable prices.

Harrods B48

Knightsbridge SW1. 071-730 1234. Most famous of British department stores, laden with Royal Warrants. Massive food halls, huge range of clothes, books, animals (stuffed, skinned and living), banking hall, travel and booking agency – in fact, everything.

HMV Record Store B39

363 Oxford St W1. 071-629 1240. One of the most comprehensive stocks of records, CDs and cassettes in London.

Liberty's B40

210–220 Regent St W1. 071-734 1234. Department store especially famous for its printed fabrics. Also particularly good on classic clothes, china, glass and fashion jewellery.

Marks & Spencer A38 & B40

173 & 458 Oxford St W1. 071-437 7722/935 7954. Two major branches of this British shopping 'institution'. Good quality clothes for adults and children. Excellent ranges of lingerie. You can't try things on but an exchange or refund is always forthcoming. Also food, books, linens, cosmetics, etc.

Selfridges B40

400 Oxford St W1. 071-629 1234. Large and hectic department store. Big food hall, huge household department; also clothes, toys, furniture and sports gear. Garage parking.

MARKETS

Wholesale markets for serious business open around dawn. Small markets for cheap fruit and veg, and 'antique' markets for bargains and rip-offs, usually open shop hours. Here are three to look at and three to shop in.

Berwick Street   **B40**
Soho W1. General market in the heart of Soho; fruit and vegetables are good, prices reasonable. *Closed Sun.*

Billingsgate (wholesale)
North Quay, West India Docks Rd, Isle of Dogs E14. The new site of London's principal fish market, moved from its age-old location in the city. Still plenty of activity. Can be wet underfoot. *Open from 05.30 Tue–Sat.*

New Covent Garden (wholesale)
Nine Elms SW8. London's foremost wholesale fruit, vegetable and flower market, moved from its Covent Garden site in 1974. *Open from 04.00–11.00 Mon–Sat.*

Petticoat Lane   **B45**
Radiates from Middlesex St E1. Huge, bustling complex selling everything under the sun; bargains, rubbish and fun. *Sun mornings only.*

Portobello Road
Nr Notting Hill Gate Underground Station W11. Famous flea market. Fruit, veg, flowers, *Mon–Sat.* Antiques, bizarre clothes and a welter of glorious junk, *Sat only.*

Smithfield (wholesale)   **B43**
Charterhouse St EC1. World's largest meat market. Interesting architecture and storage techniques but definitely not for the squeamish. *Open from 05.00–0900 Mon–Fri.*

EATING AND DRINKING

RESTAURANTS
London offers English and every kind of foreign food at all prices. The following is a brief selection. Most restaurants open *12.00–15.00, 18.00–22.30.*
For the popular national dish of fish and chips there are fish and chip shops all over London, some have tables but most do 'take away'. Add salt and vinegar and eat them from the paper wrappings in traditional style.

Archduke   **A52**
Concert Hall Approach SE1. 071-928 9370. Appealing wine bar built into a railway arch and abounding with brickwork, red pipes and hanging baskets. Plenty of wines; sausages are a speciality; French à la carte menu too. Live jazz and blues. *Closed Sat lunch & Sun.*

Cranks **B40**

8 Marshall St W1. 071-437 9431. Long established wholefood vegetarian restaurant. Self-service, cheerful, popular. *Closed Sun.*

Gallipoli **B44**

7–8 Bishopsgate Churchyard EC2. 071-588 1992. Exotic nightclub and restaurant in what was once a Victorian Turkish bath. Excellent Middle Eastern and International menu.

Geale's Fish Restaurant

2–4 Farmer St W8. 071-727 7969. Informal restaurant with cheerful service. Excellent fish and real chips, good range of starters, puddings, and wine by the glass. *Closed Sun & Mon.*

Hard Rock Café **A49**

150 Old Park Lane W1. 071-629 0382. Excellent hamburger joint with non-stop rock music. Long queues.

Khan's

13–15 Westbourne Grove W2. 071-727 5420. Vast, bustling Indian restaurant with Oriental arches. Specialities include tandoori bot kebab, kofti dilruba and mutter paneer.

Lee Ho Fook **B41**

15 Gerrard St W1. 071-734 9578. In the heart of Chinatown and much-patronised by Chinese. Excellent cooking, generous portions, but service is slow. Famous for dim sum (steamed savouries in bamboo baskets).

Maggie Jones

6 Old Court Pl, Kensington Church St W8. 071-937 6462. Cosy, pretty restaurant serving quality English cooking.

Pucci Pizza **B57**

205 King's Rd SW3. 071-352 2134. Bustling Italian restaurant with an excellent selection of pizzas and pasta, quick service and very generous portions.

San Frediano **B57**

62 Fulham Rd SW3. 071-584 8375. One of London's first Italian trattorias. Good food including excellent antipasti. A chaotic, busy and very popular restaurant.

PUBS

The pub is uniquely English and many English pubs are unique. There are historical, literary, sporting and 'theme' pubs and London has more than 7000. Here are some of the best. 🍺 – *Open all day 11.00–23.00 Mon–Sat, 12.00–14.00, 19.00–22.30 Sun.*

Where there is no 🍺 symbol the traditional hours apply – *11.00–15.00, 17.30–23.00 Mon–Sat & 12.00–14.00, 19.00–22.30 Sun.*

Cheshire Cheese, Ye Olde **B42**

145 Fleet St EC4. 071-353 6170. Rambling old building with low ceilings, oak tables and sawdusted floors above a 14thC crypt. Stout English food—famous for its winter game puddings. *Closes 21.00 and Sun.*

🍺 Dickens Inn **A55**

St Katharine's Way E1. 071-488 1226. Handsome conversion of an

historic warehouse into a pub with views over the yacht marina and towards Tower Bridge. Food on all three levels.

🍺 Dove
19 Upper Mall W6. 081-748 5405. A mellow 18thC pub with dark oak beams, soft lights, a veranda and a good view of the Thames. Large selection of snacks.

🍺 George Inn   B53
77 Borough High St SE1. 071-407 2056. London's only remaining galleried coaching inn dating from 1676. Occasional Olde Englishe style entertainments including performances of Shakespeare and Morris dancing. Two bars, wine bar and restaurant.

Jack Straw's Castle
Northend Way NW3. 071-435 8885. Lovely views over the Heath from this unusual weatherboard pub built in the 1960s. Named after Wat Tyler's closest comrade who was hanged outside an earlier pub on this site.

🍺 Lamb & Flag   A51
33 Rose St WC2. 071-497 9504. 200-year-old pub once known as 'The Bucket of Blood' when bare fist fights were held upstairs. Now a popular, mellow bar. Good lunchtime snacks and a noted strong real ale.

🍺 Mayflower
117 Rotherhithe St SE16. 071-237 4088. Tudor Inn originally called 'The Shippe', but renamed when the *Mayflower*, which set off from nearby, reached America. Licensed to sell English and US postage stamps. Nice restaurant overlooking the river.

Phoenix & Firkin
Denmark Hill Railway Station, 5 Windsor Wlk SE25. 071-701 8282. The largest and smartest pub in the *Bruce's Brewery* chain of real ale, real atmosphere pubs. Traditional in style.

🍺 Sherlock Holmes   A51
10 Northumberland St WC2. 071-930 2644. Upstairs, next to the restaurant, a reconstruction of the fictitious detective's study. Down in the bar, cuttings, curios and the head of the legendary Hound of the Baskervilles!

DINNER AND ENTERTAINMENT

Flanagan's   A38
100 Baker St W1. 071-935 0287. Phoney but enjoyable Edwardian dining rooms. Cockney songs, singing waitresses, jellied eels, game pie, fish and chips and golden syrup pudding.

Sir Christopher Wren   B43
17 Paternoster Sq, St Paul's EC4. 071-537 7447. Traditional English fayre . . . a blood curdling scream . . . a murder is announced. Dinner and mystery show in the shadows of St Paul's cathedral. No one is above suspicion – especially you!

Terrazza Est   A25
109 Fleet St EC4. 071-353 2680. Large but cosy basement restaurant with superb opera singing. Italian cuisine, lively atmosphere and lots of fun. *Open Mon–Fri to 23.00.*

Central London 2

Main Thoroughfares with Bus Routes	
Main Railway (B.R.) Stations	CHARING CROSS
Underground Railway Stations	⊖ Embankment
Places of Interest	KING'S COLLEGE
Theatres	★ APOLLO
Cinemas	● CLASSIC
Parks and Gardens	

Based upon the Ordnance Survey Maps with the sanction of the Controller of H.M. Stationery Office.

OXFORD ST.

18

WIGMORE HALL

WIGMORE ST.

WIMPOLE ST.

WELBECK ST.

WIGMORE

WELBECK ST.

WOLPOLE ST.

ROYAL COLLEGE OF MEDICINE

CAVENDISH SQ.

MARGA

PRINCES ST.

JOHN

MARYLEBONE

HENRIETTA

VERE ST.

PL. OLD CAVENDISH

HOLLES ST.

JOHN LEWIS

JAMES ST.

LA.

ST.

DERING

OXFORD NEW

HANOVER

Bond St.

S. MOLTON ST.

P.O.

SQUARE

DAVIES

ST.

GEORGE ST.

DUKE ST.

BROOK

AVERY ROW

BOND

MADDOX

CLARIDGES

STR.

SOTHEBY'S

CANADIAN HIGH COMMISSION

AEOLIAN HALL

STR.

CO

GROSVENOR SQ.

GROSVENOR

STR.

BRUTON PL.A.

ST.

CARLOS PLA.

BRUTON

P.O.

STR.

BERKELEY

GRAFTON

MOUNT

SQUARE

DOVER

BERKELEY

GATE MAYFAIR

OXFORD STREET
Oxford Street, where specially marked, is closed to through traffic (except buses and taxis) between 7a.m. and 7p.m. Monday-Saturday

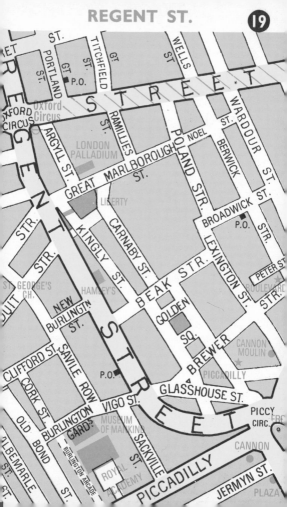

ST.

PORTLAND ST.

GT. PORTLAND ST.

TITCHFIELD

GT.

WELLS ST.

P.O.

STREET

REGENT

OXFORD CIRCUS

Oxford Circus

ARGYLL ST.

RAMILLIES ST.

LONDON PALLADIUM

GREAT MARLBOROUGH ST.

POLAND STR.

NOEL ST.

WARDOUR ST.

ST.

BERWICK ST.

LIBERTY

CARNABY ST.

BROADWICK ST.

P.O.

ST.

STR.

KINGLY ST.

LEXINGTON ST.

PETER ST.

STR.

STR.

REGENT

ST. GEORGE'S CH.

SUIT ST.

HAMLEY'S

BEAK STR.

BOULEVARD

NEW BURLINGTN ST.

GOLDEN SQ.

CANNON MOULIN

STREET

SAVILE ROW

CLIFFORD ST.

BREWER

PICCADILLY

CORK ST.

P.O.

VIGO ST.

GLASSHOUSE ST.

OLD BOND

BURLINGTON GARDS.

MUSEUM OF MANKIND

PICCY CIRC.

PICCY FRE

ALBEMARLE ST.

BURLINGTON ARCADE

SACKVILLE ST.

CANNON

ROYAL ACADEMY

PICCADILLY

JERMYN ST.

PLAZA

TROCADERO
PICCADILLY CIRCUS
EROS
CRITERION
Piccadilly Circus

COVENTRY
ST.
PR. OF WALES

ODEON
DUKE OF YORK'S
ST. MARTIN'S
LA
GARRICK

LEIC.
SQ.
IRVING ST.

ODEON WEST END

NAT. PORTRAIT GALLERY
P.C.

JERMYN ST.

HAYMARKET
PANTON ST.

ODEON
CANNON
CENTRE
CANNON
BRITISH TRAVEL CENTRE

PLAZA

REGENT STR.

P.O.

CHARLES II ST.

NEW ZEALAND HO.

CANNON
COMEDY
HAYMARKET
THEA.
ROYAL
HER MAJESTY'S

WHITCOMB ST.

NATIONAL GALLERY

TRAFALGAR

NELSON'S COLUMN

SQUARE

Ch
Cr

PALL MALL E.

CANADA HO.

COCKSPUR ST.

ST. JAMES'S SQ.

PALL MALL
GDS.
CARLTON

ROYAL AUTOMOBILE CLUB

CARLTON

MALL

WATERLOO PLACE

HO. TER.

I.C.A.

CHARING CROSS

WHITEHALL

W

ADMIRALTY ARCH

THE ADMIRALTY

THE MALL

HORSE GUARDS ROAD

GUARDS MEMORIAL

HORSE GUARDS PARADE

ST. JAMES'S PARK

DOWNING

GOVERNMENT OFFICES

COLISEUM

CHANDOS PL.

AGAR ST.

ADELPHI

VAUDEVILLE

SAVOY

CARTING LA.

WILLIAM IV. ST.

ROYAL SOCIETY OF ARTS

ST. MARTIN IN THE FIELDS

STRAND

JOHN ADAM ST.

Embankment Gdns.

CLEOPATRA'S NEEDLE

SOUTH AFRICA HO

VILLIERS

CHARING CROSS

BAND STAND

EMBANKMENT

THAMES

CRAVEN STR.

PLAYHOUSE

Embankment

NORTHUMBERLAND AV.

HUNGERFORD BRI

Gt SCOTLAND YD.

WHITEHALL PLA.

WHITEHALL CT.

Gardens

HISPANIOLA

P.S. TATTERSHALL CASTLE

(OLD WAR OFFICE)

HORSEGUARDS AV.

WHITEHALL

VICTORIA

BANQUETING HOUSE

MIN OF DEFENCE

RIVER

Jubilee Gardens

ST.

THE CENOTAPH

LONDON COUNTY HALL

SIR JOHN SOANE'S
MUSEUM

LONDON SILVER
VAULTS

LINCOLN'S INN

LINCOLNS

CHANCERY

CURSIT

Lincoln's Inn
Fields

INN

P.O.

FIELDS

OLD
CURIOSITY
SHOP

ROYAL
COLLEGE OF
SURGEONS

SERLE ST.

CAREY STR.

LANE

ROYALTY

PORTUGAL STRS.

CAREY STR.

KINGSWAY

ROYAL
COURTS
OF
JUSTICE

TEMPLE
BAR

UNDERPASS

LONDON
SCHOOL OF
ECONOMICS

P.O.

LDWYCH

ALDWYCH

AUSTRALIA
HO.

ST. CLEMENT DANES

PR.HENRY'S

MIDDLE

TRAMS

INDIA
HOUSE

STRAND

Aldwych

STRAND

ST. MARY-LE-
STRAND CH.

SURREY ST.

ARUNDEL ST.

ESSEX ST.

LANCASTER PL.

ROMAN
BATH

KING'S COLL

TEMPLE

PLA

Temple

SOMERSET HOUSE

VICTORIA

EM

UNDERPASS

HQS.
WELLINGTON
MASTER MARINERS
HALL

THAMES RIVER
POLICE STATION
WATERLOO BRI.

RIVER

PATENTS
OFFICE

HOLBORN

HOLBORN VIAT.

"DAILY MIRROR"

CITY
TEMPLE

FETTER LANE

NEW FETTER LANE

SHOE LANE

FARRINGDON ST.

ST. PAULS
THAMESLINK

RECORD
OFFICE

STONE
CUTTER
ST.

DR. JOHNSON'S HO.

GOUGH SQ.

WINE OFFICE CT.

ST. BRIDE ST.

CHESHIRE CHEESE

KIND CT.

FLEET

STREET

LUDGATE CIRCUS

LUDGTE.

P.O.

COCK TAVERN

ST. BRIDE'S CH.

SALISBURY SQUARE

BRIDE LA.

NEW BRIDGE ST.

HILL

PILGRIM

S.

TEMPLE CH. THE TEMPLE

BOURVERIE ST.

DORSET RISE

P.O.

BLACKFRIARS LA.

INNS OF COURT AND CHANCERY

TEMPLE AV.

TUDOR

STR.

JOHN CARPENTER ST.

BLACKFRIARS

BANKMENT

BLACKFRS. BRI.

H.M.S. PRESIDENT

H.M.S.
HRYSANTHEMUM

THAMES

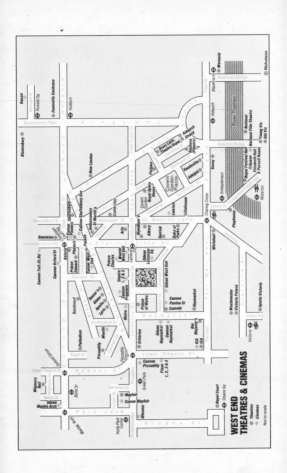

WEST END THEATRES & CINEMAS

● Theatres
● Cinemas
Not to scale

London 3

Main Thoroughfares with Bus Routes	
Main Railway (B.R.) Stations	EUSTON
Underground Railway Stations	● EMBANKMENT
Places of Interest	
Parks and Gardens	
Page Continuation Numbers	32

OXFORD STREET
Oxford Street, where specially marked, is closed to through traffic (except buses and taxis) between 7a.m. and 7p.m. Monday-Saturday

KEY MAP OVERLEAF ▶

Based upon the Ordnance Survey Maps with the sanction of the Controller of H.M. Stationery Office

KEY TO SECTIONAL

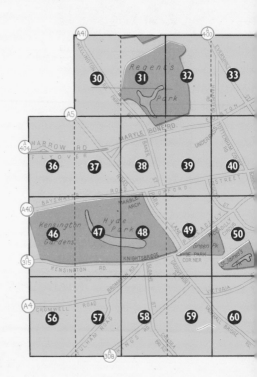

MAPS OF LONDON

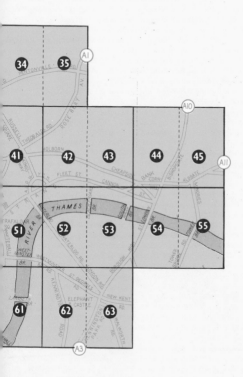

Principal Road Exits
Department of Transport Road Numbers

(A2)

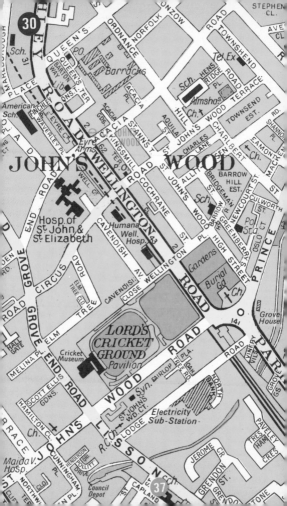

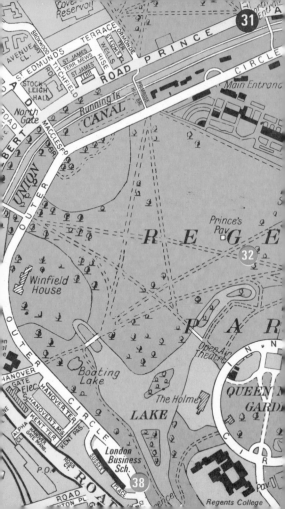

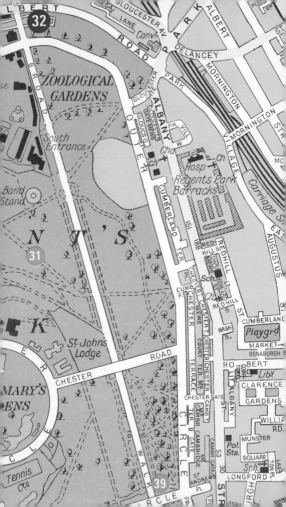

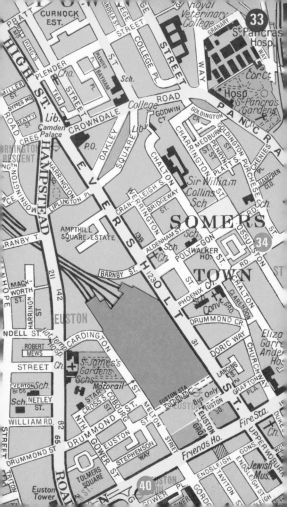

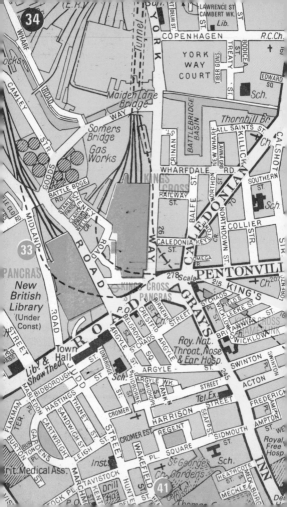

(E.R.)

LAWRENCE ST
CAMBERT WK.
Lib.

YORK COPENHAGEN R.C.Ch.

WHARF

CAMLEY

ROAD

YORK WAY COURT

BODICEA

TREATY ST

TIBER GDNS

EDWARD SQ

Sch.

Maiden Lane Bridge

WAY

Thornhill Br.

Somers Bridge Gas Works

BATTLEBRIDGE BASIN

NEW WHARF

ALL SAINTS

ANNA GRO

KILLICK

CALSHOT

GOODS

BATTLE BDGE

RD

STANFD PASS

CHENEY

RD

CRINAN

WHARFDALE

RD.

NORTHDN

SOUTHERN

Sch.

KINGS CROSS

ST.

Railway

BALFE

ST.

COLLIER

STR.

ROAD

ROYAL

MIDLAND

26

CALEDONIA

ST.

NORTHDN

KEYSE

CALEDONIAN WAY

COLLIER

STR.

PANCRAS

New British Library (Under Const)

OMEGA ST

278 Scala

PENTONVILLE

Ch. 207

215

KING'S

KINGS CROSS ST PANCRAS

GRAY'S

ST CHADS

LEEDS

WICKLOW

BRITANNIA CROSS

SAMEL WK

Town Hall

Liby & Shaw Thea.

STREET

JUDD

TONBRIDGE

BELGROVE

ST CHADS

CHESTFD

ARGYLE

SQ.

Roy. Nat. Throat, Nose & Ear Hosp.

WICKLOW

SWINTON

SWINTON

ROAD

ARGYLE

ST.

ARGYLE

ST.

THORNE

ACTON

FLAXMAN

TER.

MABLEDON

BIDBOROUGH

ST.

THANET

SANDWICH

HASTINGS

ST.

CARTWRIGHT

CROMER

ST.

ARGYLE WK

FRANT

THIRDORNE

TEL. EX.

FREDERICK

AMPTON

WE

BURTON

GARDENS

MARCHMONT

LEIGH

CROMER

ST.

HARRISON

STREET

SIDMOUTH

Royal Free Hosp

Brit. Medical Ass.

TAVISTOCK

P.O.

WAKEFIELD

REGENT

SQUARE

CROMER EST

St George's Ch. Gardens

Sch.

HEATHCOTE

MECKLENBURG

INN

Inst.

Drill Hall

HUNTER

Der

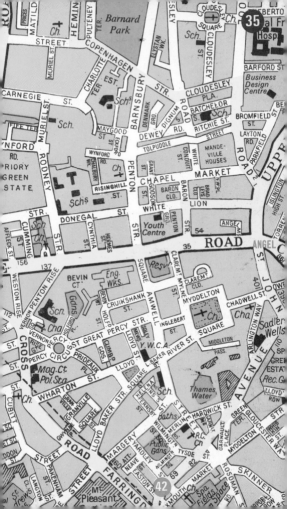

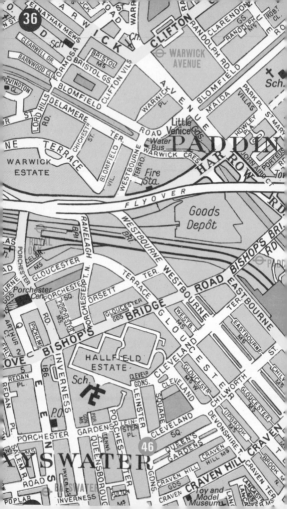

ELNATHAN MEWS

CLIFTON

WARWICK
AVENUE

CLARENDON

RANDOLPH RD.

WARWICK

CLIFTON

Ch.

WARWICK

BRISTOL MS.
BRISTOL GS.

CLEARWELL DR.

Sch.

BARNWOOD CLOSE

BLOMFIELD

CLIFTON VILS.

BLOMFIELD

MAIDA

PARK PL.

ST. MAR

ROVINGTON CL.

DELAMERE

CHICHESTER ST.

TER.

WARWICK
PL.

LORD HILLS RD.

AVENUE

BLOMFIELD

HOWLEY

VILLAS

ST. MARY

PORTE

WESTBOURNE

TERRACE

TER.

Little
Venice

Water
Bus

PADDIN

WARWICK CRES.

WARWICK
ESTATE

BLOMFIELD
VIL.

WESTBOURNE

TER. RD.

Fire
Sta.

HARRO

ROW

FLYOVER

Goods
Depôt

RANELAGH

BRI.

WESTBOURNE

BRI.

BISHOPS BRI

RD.

ROYAL
OAK

Sch.

PORCHESTER

GLOUCESTER

TERRACE

WESTBOURNE

ROAD

EASTBOURNE

PORCHESTER TER. N.

Porchester
Cen.

PORCHESTER
SQ.

ORSETT

TER.

EASTBOURNE

GLOUCESTER
MS.

ARTHUR

PICKERS

BISHOP'S

INVERNESS

GLOUCESTER
GDS.

BRIDGE

WESTB.

GLOUCESTER

CHILWORTH

TER.

GLOUCESTER

HALLFIELD
ESTATE

Sch.

CLEVELAND
GDNS.

GLOUCESTER
MS.

REDAN

186

CLEVELAND

LEINSTER

SQUARE

CLEVELO
GDNS.

CHILWORTH

REDAN
PL.

P.O.

PORCHESTER

GARDENS

LEIN-
STER
MS.

CLEVELAND
SQ.

DEVONSHIRE

UPBROOK
MS.

GLOUCESTER

SALEM R.

POPLAR

INVERNESS

QUEENSBOROUGH

QUEEN'S
GARDENS

CRAVEN
HILL
GDS.

CRAVEN
HILL

CRAVEN

BROOK

CRAVEN HILL

AYSWATER

BAYSWATER

46

Toy and
Model
Museum

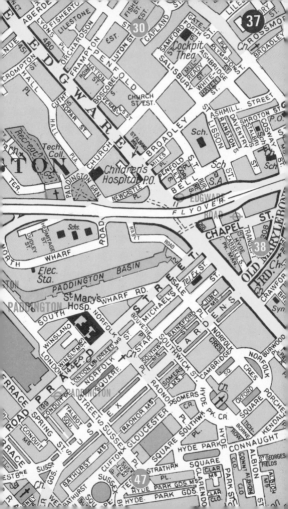

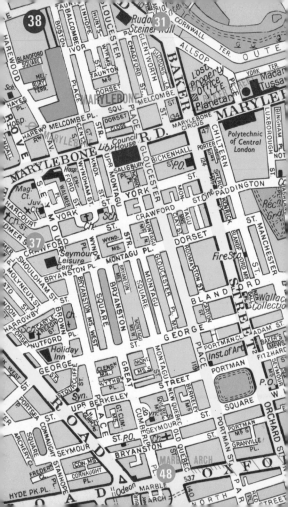

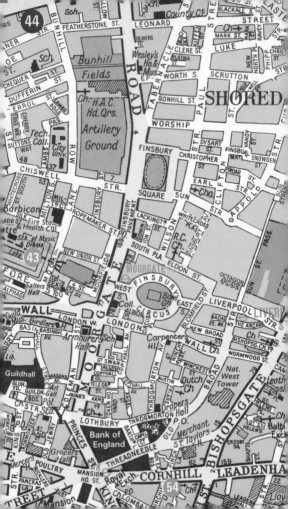

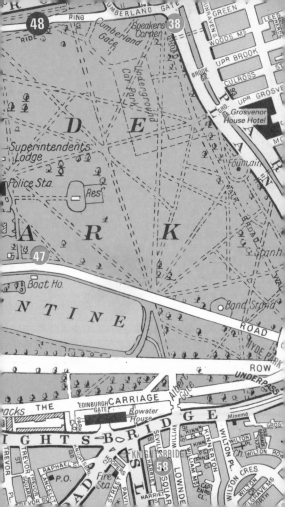

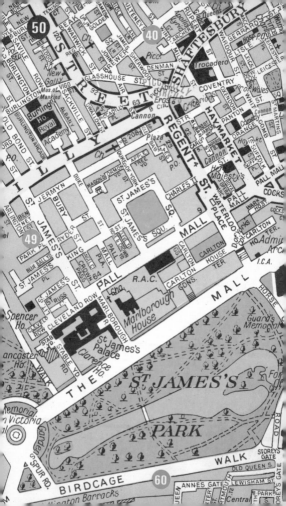

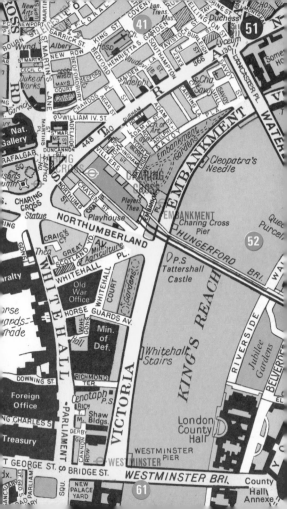

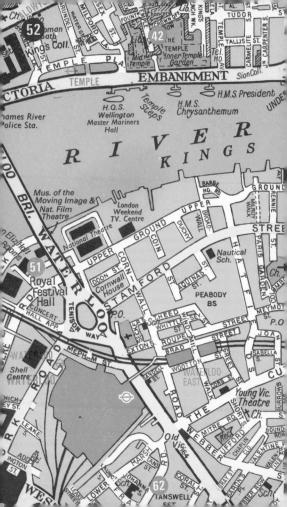

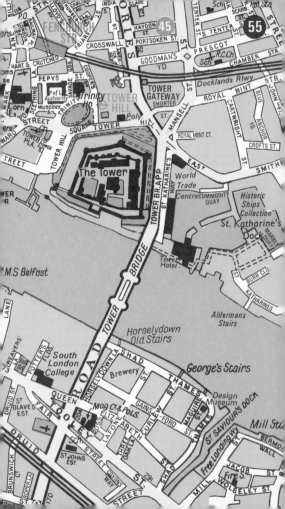

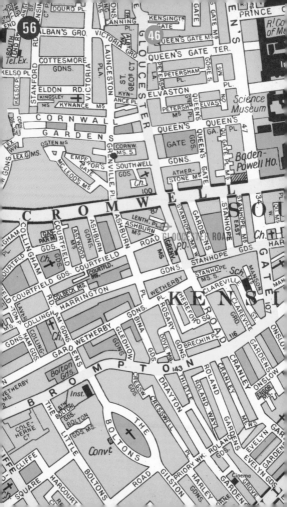

Imperial College

Science Museum

Natural History Museum

Geologic! Mus.

Victoria & Albert Museum

WATTS

PRINCES

ENNISMORE GDNS.

ENNISMORE GDS MS

ENNISMORE

MORE

MEWS

PEL

PRINCES WAY GDNS.

GDS MS

RUTLAND

CHEVAL

PRINCES GDNS MEWS

COTTAGE

BROMPTON SQUARE

OVING

OVINGTON GDNS

EGERTON

EGERTON GDNS

OVINGTON TER.

The Oratory

Ch.

CROMWELL GARDENS

PLACE

BROMPTON

ROAD

NORTH TER.

THURLOE CLO.

EGERTON GDNS.

EGERTON CRES.

EGERTON TER.

WALTON

RICHARD

MARIE

BULL

R O A D

French Sch.

CROMWELL

TH. P.
MS.

THURLOE PL.

The Ismaili Centre

THURLOE

THURLOE SQUARE

ALEXANDER PL.

SOUTH T.

SOUTH TER.

BROMPTON

58

QUEENSB

WAY

CROMWELL RD.

THURLOE ST.

SOUTH KENSINGTON

PELHAM STREET

DRAYCOTT

SLOANE

CHELSEA CLOISTERS

WALTON

DONNE

ONSLOW

BUTE ST.

PELHAM PL.

MALVERN CT.

CRES.

PELHAM PL.

LUCAN

ELYSTAN

MAKINS

PETYWARD

CRANMER

WHITE

KING-TON

Tel. Ex.

MELTON CT.

SUM. PL.
SUM. MS.

ONSLOW SQUARE

SYDNEY

PELHAM ST.

POND PL.

LEWIS TRUST BGS.

PEL.

Pol. Stn.

SUMNER PLACE

ONSLOW GDNS

Ch.

Brompton Hosp.

SYDNEY STREET

Roy. Marsden Hosp.

STEWART'S

BURY WALK

IXWORTH PL.

BORO.

SUTTON DWELLINGS

STREET

CRANLE

GDNS

ONSLOW

FULHAM

Hosp.

DOVEHOUSE ST.

DODMANSTONE

Ch.

Schs.

St. Lukes Gdns.

POMELL

C. A. E.

St. Lukes

Ct.

ASTELL

SOPHY'S

JUBILEE

WOODFALL

NEVILLE ST.

ONSLOW TER.

INST.

PARADE

SIDNEY

Schs.

GUERNSEY

OLD

SOUTH

CHELSEA SQUARE

MANRESA

BRITTEN STREET

CALE

STR.

Ch.

ELM PARK

QUEENS ELM SQ.

Thamesbrook

MANRESA ROAD

Coll.

Lib.

Polytechnic

Chelsea Cinema

P.O.

FLOOD

Ch.

Both's

24

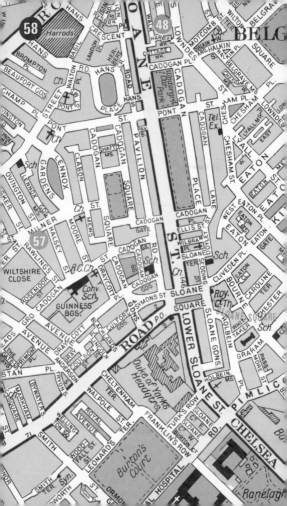

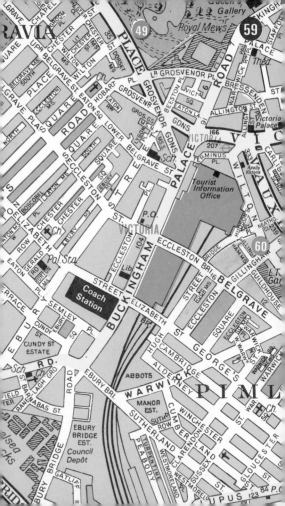

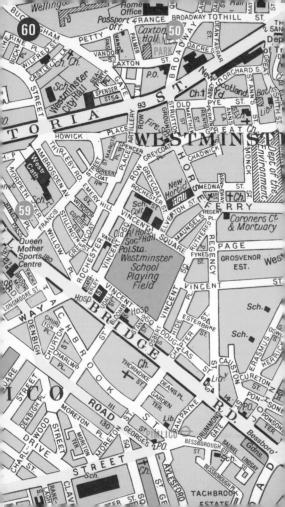

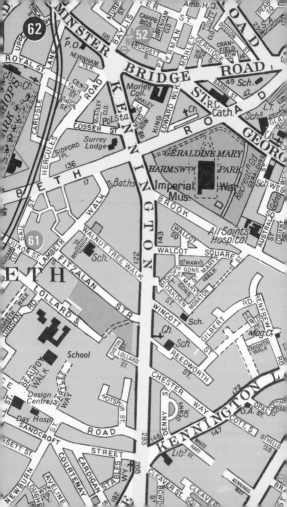

UNDERGROUND

©Copyright London Regional Transport

London Transport Underground Map Registered User Number 90/067

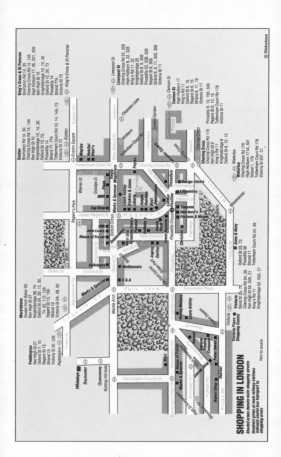

© Nicholson

Paddington
Ken High St 27
Oxford St 15
Regent St 15
Strand 15
Victoria 36, 509
Paddington ⊖ ⊜

Marylebone
(Baker Street 90)
Ken High St 27
Knightsbridge 30, 74
Oxford St 13, 135
74, 82, 113, 159
Regent St 13
Strand St 13, 159
Victoria 2, 36, 506
Victoria St 2A, 76, 82

Euston
Brompton Rd 14, 30, 14A
Charing Cross Rd 14, 14A
High Holborn 17, 45, 231, 259
Oxford St 10, 73,
Knightsbridge 10, 14, 30
Oxford St 10, 30, 73
Piccadilly 14
Tottenham Court Rd 10, 14, 14A, 73
Strand 77, 77A
Victoria St 73

King's Cross & St Pancras
Brompton 14, 30
Charing Cross Rd 14, 14A
High Holborn 17, 45, 231, 259
Knightsbridge 10, 14, 30
Oxford St 10, 30, 73
Piccadilly 14
Strand 77A
Victoria St 73

Liverpool St
Charing Cross Rd 8, 22, 239
High Holborn 8, 22, 228
Knightsbridge 22
Oxford St 6, 8, 509
Piccadilly 22, 228, 509
Regent St 6, 509
Strand 6, 8, 11, 502, 509
Victoria St 11

Cannon St
High Holborn 17
King's Rd 11
Oxford St 6, 15,
Regent St 6, 15
Strand 6, 11, 15
Victoria St 11

Charing Cross
Charing Cross Rd 176
Charing Cross Rd 176
Ken High Rd 11
King's Rd 11
Knightsbridge 9, 509
Oxford St 9, 13, 15

Waterloo
Charing Cross Rd 176
Strand 1, 176
Strand 1A, 901
Tottenham Court Rd 176
Victoria St 907, 9

Shops listed on map:
Virgin
HMV
Laura Ashley
Liberty
Aquascutum
Jaeger
Austin Reed
Dickins & Jones
Hamleys
Habitat
Heal's
Foyles
Marks & Spencer
Simpson
Fortnum & Mason
Hatchard's
John Lewis
HMV
House of Fraser
Selfridges
Mothercare
C&A
Marks & Spencel
Top Shop
Virgin
Army & Navy
Lillywhites
Design Centre
Harvey Nichols
Laura Ashley
House of Fraser
Peter Jones
Reject Shop
Habitat
Next
Whiteleys

Bond St
Bond St 25, 73
Charing Cross Rd 24, 29
Piccadilly 38
Strand 11
Tottenham Court Rd 24, 29

Victoria
Bond St 25, 73
Charing Cross Rd 24, 29
King's Rd 11
Knightsbridge 52, 52A, C1
Charing Cross Rd 176
King's Rd 11
Strand 1, 176
Tottenham Court Rd 24, 176
Victoria St 24, 52A, C1

SHOPPING IN LONDON

Shaded areas denote main shopping streets
Numbers given at most railway stations
indicate useful bus transport to
shopping areas

Not to scale

LATE & ALL NIGHT LONDON

Some useful places to know about.

LATE POST
A22
Post Office, St Martin's Pl, Trafalgar Sq WC2. 071-930 9580. *Open 08.00–20.00 Mon–Sat.*

LATE NIGHT CHEMISTS
Bliss Chemist
B38
5 Marble Arch W1. 071-723 6116. *Open 09.00–24.00 Mon–Sun.*
Boots
B19
Piccadilly Circus W1. 071-734 6126. *Open 08.30–20.00 Mon–Sat.*
Warman-Freed
45 Golders Green Rd NW11. 081-455 4351. *Open 08.00–24.00 Mon–Sun.*

LATE NIGHT RESTAURANTS
Bill Stickers
A20
18 Greek St W1. 071-437 0582. American-style fare is offered in this outrageously decorated bar/restaurant. *Open to 03.00 Mon–Sat, to 23.00 Sun.*
Canton
A51
11 Newport Pl WC2. 071-437 6220. Cantonese restaurant. *Open to 01.00 Mon–Thur & Sun, to 01.45 Fri & Sat.*
Dover Street Wine Bar
A49
8–9 Dover St W1. 071-629 9813. Live music, good food. *Open to 03.00 Mon–Sat. Closed Sun.*
Harry's
B19
19 Kingly St W1. 071-434 0309. All-night cafe serving breakfasts and snacks. Licensed. *Open all night Mon–Sat.*
Maroush I
A37
21 Edgware Rd W2. 071-723 5979. Lebanese restaurant. Meze, kebabs, grills. *Open to 02.00 Mon–Sun.*
Maroush II
A58
38 Beauchamp Pl SW3. 071-581 5434. More expensive and upmarket than Maroush I. *Open to 04.30 Mon–Sun.*
Mayflower
B20
68–70 Shaftesbury Av W1. 071-734 9207. Cantonese restaurant. *Open to 03.30 Mon–Sun.*
Up All Night
325 Fulham Rd SW10. 071-352 1996. Steaks, hamburgers and pasta in this informal restaurant. *Open to 06.00 Mon–Sat.*

NIGHTCLUBS
Listed below is a selection, check *Time Out* for others.

Busby's   **A20**
157 Charing Cross Rd WC2. 071-734 6963. Large disco with theme nights. *Open to 03.00 Mon–Sat, to 24.00 Sun.*

Empire Ballroom   **B20**
Leicester Sq WC2. 071-437 1446. Very popular. Light shows, lasers, videos in one of Europe's largest discos. *Open to 02.00 Mon–Wed, to 03.00 Thur, Fri & Sat.*

The Hippodrome   **B20**
Hippodrome Corner, nr Leicester Sq WC2. 071-437 4311. Lavishly decorated disco. Laser light show. *Open to 03.00 Mon–Sat. Closed Sun.*

Maximus   **B20**
Leicester Sq WC2. 071-734 4111. Well-established and popular with tourists. *Open to 03.00 Mon–Sun.*

Le Palais   **B20**
242 Shepherd's Bush Rd W6. 081-748 2812. Large disco with all the latest in video technology. Theme nights. *Open to 03.00 Wed–Sat. Closed Sun, Mon & Tue.*

Samantha's   **B19**
3 New Burlington St W1. 071-734 6249. Popular split-level disco with two dance floors. *Open to 03.30 Mon–Sat. Closed Sun.*

Stringfellows   **B20**
16–19 Upper St Martin's Lane WC2. 071-240 5534. Very smart restaurant and disco. *Open to 03.30 Mon–Sat. Closed Sun.*

LATE NIGHT TRANSPORT

The Underground system closes down around *midnight Mon–Sat* and *23.30 Sun.* There are all-night buses serving central London and most outer suburbs and all major routes pass through Trafalgar Square. Check with London Transport's free *24hr* Travel Information Service on 071-222 1234 for routes and times.
If you do not want to take a bus:

TAXIS

The famous black London taxi cabs can be ordered by phone or hailed in the street, they are available for hire if the yellow light above the windscreen is lit. There are over 500 ranks throughout London. For your nearest check the Phone Book under 'Taxi', or call:
Computercab: 071-286 0286.
Owner Drivers Taxi Service: 071-253 5000.
Radio Taxicabs: 071-272 0272. *24 hrs.*

MINICABS

These cannot be hailed in the street, and in any case are indistinguishable from private cars. Unlike black cabs they are not licensed but they can be cheaper on long runs and often offer *24hr* service. Negotiate the price for your journey before you start or when you phone. Your nearest minicab office is listed in the Yellow Pages.

Lady Cabs
150 Green Lanes N16. 071-254 3501. Late night cabs for women,
driven by women. *Open to 24.30 Mon–Thur, to 01.00 Fri, to 02.00
Sat, to 24.00 Sun.*

HELPFUL INFORMATION

EXCHANGING MONEY
Banks offer the best exchange rates, *open 09.30–15.30 Mon–Fri.*
Listed below are some *24hr* central London bureaux de change,
these take a higher commission.
Deak International   **B20**
15 Shaftesbury Av W1. 071-734 1400. Also at 3 Coventry St W1.
Chequepoint   **B38**
Marble Arch, 548 Oxford St W1 (071-723 2646). 58 Queensway W2
(B36). 220 Earls Court Rd SW5. 126 Bayswater Rd W2 (A36). 43
Tottenham Ct Rd W1 (A20).

CAR RENTAL
Avis Rent-a-Car   **B38**
68 North Row, Marble Arch W1. 071-629 7811. *Open 07.00–19.30.
24hr service* from Heathrow (081-897 9321) and Gatwick (0293
29721) airports.
Budget
Call 081-441 5882 for your nearest branch in London. *Open 08.30
–18.00 Mon–Fri, 09.00–12.30 Sat. Closed Sun.*
Godfrey Davis Europe Car
London Heathrow Airport. 081-897 0811. Desks in each terminal.
24hrs service.
Hertz, Rent a Car
Radnor House, 1272 London Rd SW16. 081-679 1799. Self-drive or
chauffeur-driven. Offices throughout Britain and worldwide. *Open
08.00–18.00 Mon–Fri, 08.00–17.00 Sat. Closed Sun.*
Worth Self-Drive
14 Priestly Way, Crawley RH10. (0293) 565151. Car hire for the UK.
Open 07.00–19.00 Mon–Sun.

HOTEL BOOKING AGENTS
Accommodation Service of the Tourist   **A59**
Information Centre (London Tourist Board)
Victoria Station forecourt SW1. Also at Heathrow Central Under-
ground Station. Personal callers only. Gives information and makes
hotel bookings. *Open 08.00–20.00 Mon–Sun. Easter–Oct; 09.00
–19.00 Mon–Sat & 09.00–17.00 Sun Oct–Easter.*
Concordia Worldwide Hotel Reservations   **A59**
52 Grosvenor Gdns SW1. 071-730 3467. All kinds of hotels in
London, Britain and worldwide. *Open 09.30–17.30 Mon–Fri,*

09.00–14.00 Sun. Also sales desk at Victoria Station, Platform 9.
071-828 4646. *Open 08.00–23.00 Mon–Sun.*

Expotel Hotel Reservations
Telephone booking service for hotels in Britain and worldwide. Dial
081-748 8000. *Open 08.30–18.00 Mon–Fri.*

Hotel Booking Service   B19
13–14 Golden Sq W1. 071-437 5052. Hotel reservations for the UK
and worldwide. *Open 09.30–17.30 Mon–Fri.*

Hotel Reservations Centre   B59
10 Buckingham Palace Rd SW1. 071-828 2425. Hotel reservations
made throughout the UK. *Open 08.00–18.00 Mon–Fri.* Also at
Victoria Station near Platform 8. 071-828 1027. *Open 06.00–01.00
Mon–Sun.*

Room Centre
Kingsgate House, Kingsgate Pl NW6. 071-328 1790. Booking service
for hotels in Britain and worldwide. *Open 09.00–17.30 Mon–Fri.*

LOST OR STOLEN CREDIT CARDS

During office hours the loss or theft of a credit card can be reported to
any branch of the credit card company, outside office hours contact
the *24hr* number listed and confirm by letter within seven days.

Access Card/Mastercard/Eurocard
Signet Ltd, 200 Priory Cres, Southend-on-Sea, Essex. (0702)
362988. *24hr service.*

American Express Card
Lost and Stolen Dept, American Express Company, Amex House,
Edward St, Brighton, E. Sussex. (0273) 693555. *24hr service.*

Barclaycard/Visa
Barclaycard Centre, Northampton, Northants. (0604) 234234. *24hr
service.*

Diners Club Card
Diners Club House, Kingsmead, Farnborough, Hants. (0252)
513500. *24hr service.*

LOST PROPERTY

British Rail
Contact the station where the train your belongings were lost on
terminates. They will be able to tell you where they have been taken
to.

London Transport Lost Property Office   A38
200 Baker St NW1 (next to Baker Street Underground station). Call in
in person (or send someone giving them written authority) or apply
by letter. No telephone enquiries. *Open 09.30–14.00 Mon–Fri.*

Taxis   A35
Apply to 15 Penton St N1, 071-833 0996, or nearest police station.

Lost anywhere
Apply to the nearest police station. Lost property found in the street
is usually taken there.

Index 4

ABBREVIATIONS

Arc.-Arcade
Av.-Avenue
Bldgs.-Buildings
Bri.-Bridge
Cir.-Circus
Clo.-Close
Cotts.-Cottages
Cres.-Crescent
Ct.-Court
Dr.-Drive
E.-East
Embk.-Embankment

Est.-Estate
Gdns.-Gardens
Grn.-Green
Gro.-Grove
Ho.-House
La.-Lane
Mans.-Mansions
Mkt.-Market
Ms.-Mews
N.-North
Pass.-Passage
Pk.-Park

Pl.-Place
Rd.-Road
S.-South
Sq.-Square
St.-Street
Ter.-Terrace
Upr.-Upper
Vill.-Villas
W.-West
Wk.-Walk
Yd.-Yard

Note: (1) The letters A or B precede the map page number and indicate whether the street is to be found in the upper half of the page (A), or (B) on the lower half.

(2) Certain streets named in the index are to be found in both the Central London and London map sections. In order to distinguish between the two, the name of the street that is duplicated is given first in bold type for the Central London section, followed immediately by the same name in ordinary type for the London section.

Abbey Orchard St. SW1	A60	Aldford St. W1	A49	Arlington St. SW1	A50
Abbots La. SE1	B54	Aldgate EC3	B44	Arlington Way EC1	B35
Abbots Manor Est. SW1	B59	Aldgate High St. EC3	B45	Arne St. WC2	B41
		Aldwych	**24**	Arneway St. SW1	A61
Abchurch La. EC4	A54	Aldwych WC2	A52	Arthur Ct. W2	B36
Aberdeen Pl. NW8	A37	Alexander Pl. SW7	A57	Arthur St. EC4	A54
Abingdon St. SW1	A61	Alexander Sq. SW3	A57	Artillery La. E1	A54
Acacia Gdns. NW8	A30	Alfred Ms. W1	A40	Artillery Pass. E1	B45
Acacia Pl. NW8	A30	Alfred Pl. WC1	A40	Artillery Row SW1	A59
Acacia Rd. NW8	A30	Alie St. E1	B45	Artizan St. E1	B45
Achilles Way W1	B49	All Saints St. N1	A34	**Arundel St.**	**24**
Acton St. WC1	B34	All Souls Pl. W1	B39	Arundel St. WC2	A52
Adam & Eve Ct. W1	B40	Allhallows La. EC4	A54	Ash Pl. SW1	A59
Adam St.	**21**	Allington St. SW1	A59	Ashbridge St. NW8	A37
Adam St. W1	B38	Allitsen Rd. NW8	A30	Ashburn Gdns. SW7	A56
Adam St. WC2	A51	Allsop Pl. NW1	A38	Ashburn Ms. SW7	A56
Adams Row W1	A49	Alpha Clo. NW1	B31	Ashburn Pl. SW7	A56
Addington St. SE1	B52	Ambergate St. SE17	B63	Ashland Pl. W1	A38
Addle Hill EC4	B43	Amelia St. SE17	B63	Ashmill St. NW1	A37
Adelaide St.	**23**	Amen Ct. EC4	B43	Assam St. E1	B45
Adelaide St. WC2	A51	America Sq. EC3	A55	Astell St. SW3	B57
Adeline Pl. WC1	B40	America St. EC1	B53	Aster Pl. SE1	B58
Adelphi Ter. WC2	A51	Ampthill Square Est. NW1	A33	Astwood Ms. SW7	A56
Adpar St. W2	A37			Atherstone Ms. SW7	B58
Affleck St. N1	A35	Ampton Pl. WC1	B34	Atterbury St. SW1	B61
Agar St.	**21**	Ampton St. WC1	B34	Attneave St. WC1	B35
Agar St. WC2	A51	Amwell St. EC1	B35	Auden Pl. NW1	A30
Air St. W1	B50	Anderson St. SW8	B58	Audley St. W1	A58
Albany St. NW1	B32	Angel Ct. EC2	B44	Augustus St. NW1	B32
Albany Ter. NW1	B32	Angel Ct. SW1	B50	Austin Friars EC2	B44
Albany, The W1	A50	Angel Ms. N1	A35	Austral St. SE11	B62
Albemarle St.	**19**	Angel Pl. EC4	B54	Ave Maria La. EC4	A54
Albemarle St. W1	A49	Angel Pl. SE1	A54	Aveline St. SE11	B62
Albert Embk. SE1	B61	Angel St. EC1	B43	Avenue Clo. NW8	A31
Albert Hall Ms. SW7	A57	Anns Clo. SW1	B48	Avenue Rd. NW8	A31
Albert Ms. W8	A57	Ansdell St. W8	A46	Avenue, The EC3	A54
Albert Pl. W8	A57	Ansdell Ter. W8	A46	**Avery Row**	**18**
Albert St. NW1	A32	Appletree Yd. SW1	A50	Avery Row W1	A49
Albert Ter. NW1	A31	Appold St. EC2	A44	Avon Pl. SE1	A63
Albert Terrace Ms. NW1	A31	Aquila St. NW8	A30	Avonmouth St. SE1	A63
		Aquinas St. SE1	B52	Aybrook St. W1	A39
Alberta Est. SE17	B63	Arcade, The EC2	B44	Aylesbury Rd. SE17	B63
Alberta St. SE17	B63	Arch St. SE1	A63	Aylesbury St. EC1	A43
Albion Ms. W2	B37	Archer St. W1	A50	Aylesford St. SW1	B60
Albion Pl. EC1	A43	Archery Clo. W2	B38	Ayres St. SE1	B53
Albion St. W2	B37	Argent St. SE1	B53	Babmaes St. SW1	A50
Aldenham St. NW1	A33	Argyle St. WC1	B34	Back Gravel La. E1	B45
Aldermanbury EC2	B43	Argyle Wk. WC1	B34	Back Hill, EC1	A42
Aldermanbury Sq. EC2	B43	Argyll St. W1	B40	Baden Pl. SE1	A54
Alderney St. SW1	B59	Arlington Rd. NW1	A33	Bainbridge St. WC1	B41
Alders Gate EC1	A43	Arlington Sq. N1	A50	Baker St. NW1	A38
				Bakers Ms. W1	B38

Bakers Row EC1   A52
Balcombe St. NW1   A38
Balderton St. W1   A38
Baldwins Gdns. EC1   A42
Balfe St. N1   A34
Balfour Ms. W1   A48
Balfour Pl. W1   A48
Balniel Gate SW1   B60
Baltic St. EC1   A43
Bankend SE1   B53
Bankside SE1   A52
Bankside SE1   B53
Banner St. EC1   A43
Barbel St. SE1   A62
Barge House Rd. SE1   A52
Bark Pl. W1   A46
Barlow Pl. W1   A49
Barnby St. NW1   B33
Barnham St. SE1   B54
Barnsbury Rd. N1   A35
Barnwood Clo. W9   A36
Baron Clo. N1   A35
Baron St. N1   A35
Barons Pl. SE1   B52
Barrett St. W1   B39
Barrie Est. W2   A47
Barron Clo. WC1   A41
Barrow Hill Est. NW8   A30
Barrow Hill NW8   A30
Barter St. WC1   B41
Bartholomew Clo. EC1   A43
Bartholomew La. EC2   B44
Bartlett Ct. EC4   B42
Barton St. SW1   A61
Barton Way NW8   A30
Basil St. SW3   A58
Basinghall Av. EC2   B43
Basinghall St. EC2   B43
Bastwick St. EC1   A43
Batchelor St. N1   A35
Bateman St. W1   B40
Bath Ct. EC1   A42
Bath Ter. SE1   A63
Bathurst Ms. W2   B37
Bathurst St. W2   B37
Batt Ms. NW1   A33
Batt St. NW1   A33
Battle Bridge La. SE1   B54
Battle Bridge Rd. NW1   A34
Bayham Pl. NW1   A33
Bayham St. NW1   A33
Bayley St. WC1   B40

Baylis Rd. SE1   A62
Bayswater Rd. W2   A46
Beak St.   **19**
Beak St. W1   A50
Bear Alley EC4   B43
Bear Gdns. SE1   A53
Bear La. SE1   B53
Bear St. WC2   A50
Beatty St. NW1   A33
Beauchamp Pl. SW3   A57
Beauchamp St. EC1   A42
Beaufort Gdns. SW3   A58
Beaufoy Wk. SE11   B62
Beaumont Ms. W1   A39
Beaumont Pl. W1   A40
Beaumont St. W1   A39
Bedale St. SE1   B54
Bedford Av. WC1   B40
Bedford Ct. WC2   A51
Bedford Pl. WC1   A41
Bedford Row WC1   A42
Bedford Sq. WC1   A40
Bedford St.   **21**
Bedford St. WC2   A51
Bedford Way WC1   A41
Bedfordbury WC2   A51
Beech St. EC2   A43
Beeston Pl. SW1   A59
Belgrave Ms. N. SW1   A48
Belgrave Ms. S. SW1   A59
Belgrave Ms. W. SW1   A58
Belgrave Pl. SW1   A59
Belgrave Rd. SW1   B59
Belgrave Sq. SW1   A58
Belgrove St. WC1   B34
Bell La. E1   B45
Bell St. NW1   A37
Bell Yd. WC2   B42
Belvedere Bldgs. SE1   B53
Belvedere Pl. SE1   A63
Belvedere Rd. SE1   A61
Bemerton St. N1   A34
Bendall Ms. NW1   A38
Benjamin St. EC1   A43
Bennet St. SW1   A50
Bentinck Ms. W1   B39
Bentinck St. W1   B39
Berkeley Ms. W1   B38
Berkeley Sq.   **18**
Berkeley Sq. W1   A49
Berkeley St.   **18**
Berkeley St. W1   A49

Bermondsey St. SE1   B54
Bernard St. WC1   A41
Berners Ms. W1   B40
Berners Pl. W1   B40
Berners Rd. N1   A35
Berners St. W1   B40
Berry St. EC1   A43
Berryfield Rd. SE17   B63
Berwick St.   **19**
Berwick St. W1   B40
Bessborough Gdns. SW1   B60
Bessborough Pl. SW1   B60
Bessborough St. SW1   B60
Bessborough Way SW1   B60
Bethnal Green Rd. E1   A45
Betterton St. WC2   B41
Bevin Ct. WC1   B35
Bevin Way WC1   B35
Bevis Marks EC3   B45
Bickenhall St. W1   A38
Bidborough St. WC1   B34
Billiter St. EC3   A55
Bina Gdns. SW5   B56
Bingham Pl. W1   A38
Binney St. W1   B39
Birchin La. EC3   B44
Bird St. W1   B39
Birdcage Wk. SW1   B50
Birkenhead St. WC1   B34
Bishops Bridge Rd. W2   B36
Bishops Ct. EC4   B43
Bishops Ct. WC2   B42
Bishops Ter. SE11   B62
Bishopsgate Church Yd. EC2   B44
Bishopsgate EC2   B44
Bittern St. SE1   B53
Black Prince Rd. SE11   B61
Blackburnes Ms. W1   A48
Blackfriars Bri.   **25**
Blackfriars Bri. EC4   A53
Blackfriars La.   **25**
Blackfriars La. EC4   A53
Blackfriars Pass. EC4   A53
Blackfriars Rd. SE1   A62
Blacklands Ter. SW3   B58
Blandford Ms. W1   A38
Blandford Sq. NW1   A38
Blandford St. W1   B38
Blenheim St. W1   B39

Blomfield Rd. W9	A36
Blomfield St. EC2	B44
Blomfield Vill. W2	A36
Bloomburg St. SW1	B60
Bloomfield Ter. SW1	B58
Bloomsbury Pl. WC1	A41
Bloomsbury Sq. WC1	A41
Bloomsbury St. WC1	B41
Bloomsbury Way WC1	B41
Blossom St. E1	A45
Blue Anchor Yd. E1	A55
Blue Ball Yd. SW1	B50
Boadicea St. N1	A34
Bolsover St. W1	A39
Bolt Ct. EC4	B42
Bolton Gardens Ms. SW10	B56
Bolton Gdns. SW5	B56
Bolton St. W1	A50
Bolton, The SW10	B56
Bonhill St. EC2	A44
Booths Pl. W1	B40
Borers St. E1	A55
Borough High St. SE1	A63
Borough Rd. SE1	A63
Boscobel Pl. SW1	A59
Boscobel St. NW8	A37
Boss St. SE1	B55
Boston Pl. NW1	A38
Boswell Ct. WC1	A41
Boswell St. WC1	A41
Botolph La. EC3	B44
Boundary Row SE1	B52
Bourchier St. W1	B40
Bourdon Pl. W1	A49
Bourdon St. W1	A49
Bourlet Clo. W1	B40
Bourne Est. EC1	A42
Bourne St. SW1	B58
Bourne Ter. W2	A36
Bouverie Pl. W2	B37
Bouverie St.	**25**
Bouverie St. EC4	B42
Bow La. EC4	B43
Bow St.	**21**
Bow St. WC2	B41
Bowden St. SE11	B62
Bowling Green La. EC1	A42
Bowling Green Pl. SE1	B54
Boyfield St. SE1	B53
Boyle St. W1	A49
Brackley St. EC1	A43
Brad St. SE1	B52
Braden St. W9	A36
Bradleys Clo. N1	A35
Braganza St. SE17	B62
Braham St. E1	B45
Braidwood St. SE1	B54
Bramham Gdns. SW5	B56
Brandon Rd. SE17	A63
Brandon St. SE17	B63
Brangton Rd. SE11	B62
Bray Pl. SW3	B58
Bread St. EC4	B43
Breams Bldgs. EC4	B42
Brechin Pl. SW7	B56
Bremen Rd. SW7	B46
Brendon St. W1	B37
Bressenden Pl. SW1	A59
Brew House Yd. EC1	A43
Brewer St.	**19**
Brewer St. W1	A50
Brick St. W1	B49
Bride La.	**25**
Bridewell Pl. EC4	B42
Bridford Ms. W1	A39
Bridge Pl. SW1	B59
Bridge St. SW1	B51
Bridge Yd. SE1	B54
Bridgeman St. NW8	A30
Bridgewater Highwalk EC1	A43
Bridgewater Sq. EC2	A43
Bridgewater St. EC2	A43
Bridgeway St. NW1	A33
Bridle La. W1	A50
Briset St. EC1	A43
Bristol Gdns. W9	A36
Bristol Ms. W9	A36
Britannia St. WC1	B34
Britten St. SW3	B57
Britton St. EC1	A43
Broad Ct. WC2	B41
Broad Sanctuary SW1	B51
Broad St. W1	A49
Broad Street Av. EC2	B44
Broad Wk. NW1	A32
Broad Wk. W1	A48
Broad Wk., The W8	A46
Broad Yd. EC1	A42
Broadbent St. W1	A49
Broadley Portman Bldgs. NW1	A31
Bradley St. NW8	A37
Broadwall SE1	A52
Broadway SW1	A60
Broadwick St.	**19**
Broadwick St. W1	B40
Brockham St. SE1	A63
Bromfield St. N1	A35
Brompton Pl. SW3	A58
Brompton Rd. SW3	B56
Brompton Sq. SW3	A57
Bronti Clo. SE17	B63
Brook Dr. SE11	A62
Brook Gate W1	A48
Brook Ms. W2	B36
Brook St.	**18**
Brook St. W1	A49
Brook St. W2	B37
Brooke St. EC1	A42
Brookes Ct. EC1	A42
Brooks Ms. W1	A49
Brown Hart Gdns. W1	B38
Browning Est. SE17	A63
Browning Ms. W1	A39
Browning St. SE17	A63
Brownlow Ms.WC1	A42
Brownlow St. WC1	A42
Broxwood Way NW8	A31
Brune St. E1	B45
Brunswick Ct. SE1	B55
Brunswick Sq. WC1	A41
Brushfield St. E1	B45
Bruton La. W1	A49
Bruton Pl.	**18**
Bruton Pl. W1	A49
Bruton St.	**18**
Bruton St. W1	A49
Bryanston Ms. E. W1	B38
Bryanston Ms. W. W1	B38
Bryanston Pl. W1	B38
Bryanston Sq. W1	B38
Bryanston St. W1	B38
Buckingham Gate SW1	B59
Buckingham Palace Rd. SW1	B59
Buckingham Pl. SW1	B59
Buckingham St. WC2	B59
Buckle St. E1	B45
Buckler St. EC4	B44
Bucklersbury EC4	B44
Bucknall St. WC2	B41
Budge Row EC4	A54
Bull Wharf La. EC4	A53

74

Bulls Gdns. SW3	A57
Bulls Head Pl. EC3	B44
Bulstrode Pl. W1	B39
Bulstrode St. W1	B39
Bunhill Row EC1	A44
Burdett St. SE1	A62
Burk Wk. SW3	B57
Burleigh St. WC2	A51
Burlington Arc.	**19**
Burlington Arc. W1	A50
Burlington Gdns.	**19**
Burlington Gdns. W1	A50
Burman St. SE1	A63
Burne St. NW1	A37
Burnsall St. SW3	B57
Burr Clo. E1	B55
Burrell St. SE1	B53
Burrows Ms. SE1	B52
Burton Ms. SW1	B59
Burton Pl. WC1	B34
Burton St. WC1	B34
Burwood Pl. W2	B37
Bury Ct. EC3	B45
Bury St. EC3	B45
Bury St. SW1	A50
Bush La. EC4	A54
Bute St. SW7	A57
Buxton St. E1	A45
Byng Pl. WC1	A40
Byward St. EC3	A53
Bywater St. SW3	B58
Cabell St. NW1	A37
Cadogan Gate SW1	A58
Cadogan Gdns. SW1	A58
Cadogan La. SW1	A58
Cadogan Pl. SW1	A58
Cadogan Sq. SW1	A58
Cadogan St. SW3	B58
Cale St. SW3	B57
Caleb St. SE1	B53
Caledonia St. N1	A34
Caledonian Rd. N1	B34
Calshot St. N1	A34
Calthorpe St. WC1	A42
Calvin St. E1	A45
Cambert Wk. NW1	A34
Cambridge Cir.	**20**
Cambridge Cir. WC2	B40
Cambridge Gate Ms. NW1	B32
Cambridge Gate NW1	B32
Cambridge Pl. W8	B46

Cambridge Sq. W2	B37
Cambridge St. SW1	B59
Cambridge Ter. NW1	B32
Cambridge Terrace Ms. NW1	B32
Camden High St. NW1	A32
Camden St. NW1	A33
Camlet St. E2	A45
Camley St. NW1	A34
Camomile St. EC3	B44
Campbell Bldgs. SE1	A62
Camperdown St. E1	B45
Candover St. W1	A40
Canning Ms. W8	A56
Canning Pass. W8	B46
Canning Pl. W8	A56
Cannon Row SW1	B51
Cannon St. EC4	B43
Canvey St. SE1	A53
Capel Ct. EC2	B44
Capland St. NW8	A37
Capper St. WC1	A40
Carburton St. W1	A39
Cardigan St. SE11	B62
Cardington St. NW1	B33
Carey La. EC2	B43
Carey St.	**24**
Carey St. WC2	B42
Carlisle Av. EC3	A55
Carlisle La. SE1	A62
Carlisle Pl. SW1	A59
Carlisle St. W1	B40
Carlos Pl.	**18**
Carlos Pl. W1	A49
Carlton Gdns.	**22**
Carlton Gdns. SW1	B50
Carlton House Ter.	**22**
Carlton House Ter. SW1	B50
Carlton St. SW1	A50
Carlyle Sq. SW3	B57
Carmelite St. EC4	A52
Carnaby St.	**19**
Carnaby St. W1	B40
Carnegie St. N1	A35
Caroline Pl. W2	A46
Caroline Ter. SW1	B58
Carpenter St. W1	A49
Carpenters Clo. SW1	B48
Carrington St. W1	B49
Carter La. EC4	B43
Carter St. SW1	B50

Carthusian St. EC1	A43
Carting La.	**21**
Carting La. WC2	A51
Carton St. W1	B38
Cartwright Gdns. WC1	B34
Cartwright St. E1	A55
Casson St. E1	B45
Castellain Rd. W9	A36
Castle La. SW1	A60
Castle St. EC1	A42
Castlereagh St. W1	B38
Cathedral Pl. EC4	B43
Cathedral St. SE1	B54
Catherine Pl. SW1	A60
Catherine St.	**21**
Catherine St. WC2	B41
Cato St. W1	B38
Catton St. WC1	B41
Causton St. SW1	B60
Cavaye Pl. SW10	B56
Cavendish Av. NW8	A30
Cavendish Clo. NW8	A30
Cavendish Pl. W1	B39
Cavendish Sq.	**18**
Cavendish Sq. W1	B39
Caxton St. SW1	A60
Cecil Ct. WC2	A51
Celbridge Ms. W2	B36
Centaur St. SE1	A62
Central Mkts. EC1	B43
Cerney Ms. W2	B37
Chadwell St. EC1	B35
Chadwick St. SW1	A60
Chagford St. NW1	A38
Chalbury Wk. N1	A35
Chalton St. NW1	A33
Chamber St. E1	A55
Chambers St. SE16	B55
Chance St. E2	A45
Chancel St. SE1	B53
Chancery La.	**24**
Chancery La. WC2	B42
Chandos Pl.	**21**
Chandos Pl. WC2	A51
Chandos St. W1	B39
Chapel Mkt. N1	A35
Chapel Pl. W1	B39
Chapel St. NW1	A37
Chapel St. SW1	A59
Chaplin Clo. SE1	B52
Chapter St. SW1	B60

Charing Cross	22	Chester Terrace Ms.	B32	Clarges St. W1	A49
Charing Cross Rd.	20	NW1		Claverton St. SW1	B60
Charing Cross Rd.	B40	Chester Way SE11	B62	Clay St. W1	A38
WC2		Chesterfield Gdns. W1	A49	Clearwell Dr. W9	A36
Charing Cross WC2	A51	Chesterfield Hill W1	A49	Cleaver Sq. SE11	B62
Charlbert St. NW8	A30	Chesterfield St. W1	A49	Cleaver St. SE11	B62
Charles II St.	22	Cheval Pl. SW7	A57	Cleeve Yd. SW1	A50
Charles II St. SW1	A50	Chicheley St. SE1	B51	Clements Inn Pass.	B42
Charles La. W1	A49	Chichester Rents WC2	B42	WC2	
Charleston St. SE17	B63	Chichester St. SW1	B60	Clements Inn WC2	B42
Charlotte Pl. W1	B40	Chichester St. W2	A36	Clements La. EC4	B42
Charlotte Rd. EC2	A44	Chicksand Est. E1	A45	Clennam St. SE1	B53
Charlotte Ter. N1	A35	Chicksand St. E1	B45	Clere Pl. EC2	A44
Charlwood Pl. SW1	B60	Chiltern St. W1	A38	Clere St. EC2	A44
Charlwood St. SW1	B60	Chilton St. E2	A45	Clerkenwell Clo. EC1	A42
Charrington St. NW1	A33	Chilworth Ms. W2	B36	Clerkenwell Grn. EC1	A42
Charterhouse Bldgs.	A43	Chilworth St. W2	B36	Clerkenwell Rd. EC1	A42
EC1		Chiswell St. EC1	A44	Clerks Pl. EC3	B44
Charterhouse Ms. EC1	A43	Chitty St. W1	A40	Cleveland Gdns. W2	B36
Charterhouse Sq. EC1	A43	Christina St. EC2	A44	Cleveland Ms. W1	A40
Charterhouse St. EC1	A43	Christopher St. EC2	A44	Cleveland Row SW1	B50
Charterhouse St. EC1	B42	Church St. W2	A37	Cleveland Sq. W2	B36
Cheapside EC2	B43	Church Street Est.	A37	Cleveland St. W1	A39
Chelsea Bridge Rd.	A58	NW8		Cleveland Ter. W2	B36
SW1		Church Yard Row	B63	**Clifford St.**	19
Chelsea Cloisters SW3	B57	SE11		Clifford St. W1	A49
Chelsea Manor Gdns.	B57	Churchway NW1	B33	Clifton Ct. NW8	B30
SW3		Churton Pl. SW1	B60	Clifton Gdns. W9	A36
Chelsea Manor St.	B57	Churton St. SW1	B60	Clifton Rd. W9	A36
SW3		Circular Rd. SE1	A63	Clifton St. EC2	A44
Chelsea Sq. SW3	B57	Circus Pl. EC2	B44	Clifton Ter. W2	B37
Cheltenham Ter. SW3	B58	Circus Rd. NW8	B30	Clifton Vill. W9	A36
Cheney Rd. NW1	A34	City Rd. EC1	A44	Clink St. SE1	A54
Chenies Pl. NW1	A33	City Rd. EC1	B35	Clipstone Ms. W1	A40
Chenies St. WC1	A40	Clabon Ms. SW1	A58	Clipstone St. W1	A39
Chequer St. EC1	A44	Clare Mkt. WC2	B41	Cliveden Pl. SW1	B58
Cherry Tree Wk. EC1	A44	Claremont Clo. N1	B35	Cloak La. EC4	A54
Chesham Ms. SW1	A58	Claremont Sq. N1	B35	Clock Pl. SE1	B63
Chesham Pl. SW1	A58	Clarence Gdns. NW1	B32	Cloth Fair EC1	B43
Chesham St. SW1	A58	Clarence Pass. NW1	A34	Cloudesley Pl. N1	A35
Cheshire Clo. E2	A45	Clarence Ter. NW1	A38	Cloudesley Rd. N1	A35
Cheshire St. E2	A45	Clarence Yd. SE17	B63	Cloudesley Sq. N1	A35
Chester Clo. SW1	B49	Clarendon Clo. W2	B37	Cloudesley St. N1	A35
Chester Ct. NW1	B32	Clarendon Gdns. W9	A36	Club Row E2	A45
Chester Gate NW1	B32	Clarendon Gro. NW1	B33	Coach & Horses Yd.	A49
Chester Ms. SW1	A39	Clarendon Ms. W2	B37	W1	
Chester Pl. NW1	B32	Clarendon Pl. W2	B37	Cobb St. E1	B45
Chester Rd. NW1	B32	Clarendon St. SW1	B59	Coburg Clo. SW1	A60
Chester Row SW1	B58	Clarendon Ter. W9	A36	Coburg St. NW1	B33
Chester Sq. SW1	A59	Clareville Gro. SW7	B56	Cochrane St. NW8	A30
Chester St. SW1	A59	Clareville St. SW7	B56	Cock La. EC1	B43
Chester Ter. NW1	B32	Clarges Ms. W1	A49		

76

Cockpit Yd. WC1   A42
Cockspur Ct. SW1   A50
Cockspur St.   **22**
Cockspur St. SW1   A50
Code St. E1   A45
Coin St. SE1   A52
Colbeck Ms. SW7   B56
Colchester St. E1   B45
Coldbath St. EC1   A42
Cole St. SE1   B54
Coleherne Ct. SW5   B56
Coleman St. EC2   B44
Coley St. WC1   A42
College Gro. NW1   A33
College Hill EC4   A54
College Pl. NW1   A33
College Pl. EC4   A54
College St. NW1   A33
Collier St. N1   A34
Collingham Gdns. SW5   B56
Collingham Pl. SW5   A56
Collingham Rd. SW5   A56
Colnbrook St. SE1   A62
Colombo St. SE1   B52
Colonnade WC1   A41
Colville Pl. W1   A40
Colworth Gro. SE17   B63
Commercial Rd. E1   B45
Commercial St. E1   A45
Commodity Quay E1   A55
Compton Clo. NW1   B32
Compton Pass. EC1   A43
Compton St. EC1   A43
Concert Hall App. SE1   B52
Conduit Ms. W2   B37
Conduit Pl. W2   B37
Conduit St.   **18**
Conduit St. W1   A49
Connaught Clo. W2   B37
Connaught Pl. W2   B38
Connaught Sq. W2   B38
Connaught St. W2   B37
Cons St. SE1   B52
Constitution Hill SW1   B49
Content St. SE17   B63
Conway Ms. W1   A39
Cooper Clo. SE1   A62
Coopers La. WC1   A34
Coopers Row EC3   A55
Copenhagen St. N1   A34
Copenhagen St. N1   A35

Copperfield St. SE1   B53
Copthall Av. EC2   B44
Copthall Clo. EC2   B44
Coptic St. WC1   B41
Coral St. SE1   B52
Coram St. WC1   A41
Corbet Pl. E1   A45
Cork St.   **19**
Cork St. W1   A49
Corlett St. NW1   A37
Cornhill EC3   B44
Cornwall Gardens Wk. SW7   A56
Cornwall Gdns. SW7   A56
Cornwall Ms. S. SW7   A56
Cornwall Rd. SE1   A52
Cornwall Ter. NW1   A38
Corporation Row EC1   A42
Cosmo Pl. WC1   A41
Cosser St. SE1   A62
Cosway St. NW1   A37
Cotham St. SE17   B63
Cottage Pl. SW3   A57
Cottage Wk. SW1   A58
Cottesmore Gdns. W8   A56
Cottington Clo. SE11   B62
Cottington St. SE11   B62
Cotton La. SE1   B54
Coulson St. SW3   B58
Courtenay St. SE11   B62
Courtfield Gdns. SW5   B56
Courtfield Ms. SW7   B56
Courtfield Rd. SW7   B56
Cousin La. EC4   A54
Covent Gdn.   **21**
Covent Gdn. WC2   A51
Coventry St.   **20**
Coventry St. W1   A50
Cowcross St. EC1   A42
Cowley St. SW1   A61
Cowper St. EC2   A44
Coxons Way SW1   B55
Coxs Ct. EC1   B43
Coxson Pl. SE1   B55
Craigs Ct. SW1   A51
Cramer St. W1   A39
Crampton St. SE17   B63
Cranbourn St.   **20**
Cranbourn St. WC2   A50
Cranfield Row SE1   A62
Cranleigh St. NW1   A33
Cranley Gdns. SW7   B56

Cranley Ms. SW7   B56
Cranley Pl. SW7   B57
Cranmer Ct. SW3   B57
Craven Hill Gdns. W2   B36
Craven Hill Ms. W2   B36
Craven Hill W2   B36
Craven Pl. WC2   A51
Craven Rd. W2   B36
Craven St.   **23**
Craven St. WC2   A51
Craven Ter. W2   B36
Crawford Pass. EC1   A42
Crawford Pl. W1   B37
Crawford St. W1   A38
Crawford St. W1   B38
Creechurch La. EC3   A45
Creed La. EC4   B43
Crescent Row EC1   A43
Crescent, The EC3   A55
Cresswell Gdns. SW5   B56
Cresswell Pl. SW10   B56
Crestfield St. WC1   B34
Crinan St. N1   A34
Cripplegate St. EC1   A43
Crispin St. E1   B45
Crofts St. E1   A55
Cromer Est. WC1   B34
Cromer St. WC1   B34
Crompton St. W2   A37
Cromwell Gdns. SW7   A57
Cromwell Pl. SW7   A57
Cromwell Rd. SW7   A56
Crosby Row SE1   B54
Crosby Sq. EC3   B44
Cross Keys Clo. W1   B39
Crosswall EC3   A55
Crown Ct. WC2   A41
Crown Office Row EC4   A52
Crown Pass. SW1   B50
Crowndale Rd. NW1   A33
Crucifix La. SE1   B54
Cruikshank St. WC1   B35
Crutched Friars EC3   A55
Cubitt St. WC1   B35
Culford Gdns. SW1   B58
Cullum St. EC3   A54
Culross St. W1   A48
Culworth St. NW8   A30
Cumberland Gate W1   B38
Cumberland Gdns. WC1   B35

Cumberland Mkt. NW1	B32
Cumberland Pl. NW1	B32
Cumberland St. SW1	B59
Cumberland Ter. NW1	A32
Cumming St. N1	A35
Cundy St. SW1	B59
Cundy Street Est. SW1	B59
Cunningham Pl. NW8	B30
Cureton St. SW1	B60
Curlew St. SE1	B55
Curnock Est. NW1	A33
Cursitor St.	**24**
Cursitor St. EC4	B42
Curtain Rd. EC2	A44
Curzon Gate W1	B49
Curzon Pl. W1	B49
Curzon St. W1	B49
Cut, The SE1	B52
Cuthbert St. W2	A37
Cutler St. E1	B45
Cynthia St. N1	A35
Cypress Pl. W1	A40
Cyprus St. EC1	A43
D'arblay St. W1	B40
Dacre St. SW1	A60
Dallington St. EC1	A43
Dane St. WC1	B41
Dante Pl. SE11	B63
Dante Rd. SE11	B63
Danube St. SW3	B57
Daplyn St. E1	A45
Dartmouth St. SW1	A60
Daventry St. NW1	A37
David Ms. W1	A38
Davidge St. SE1	A63
Davies Ms. W1	B39
Davies St.	**18**
Davies St. W1	B40
De Vere Gdns. W8	B46
De Waldon St. W1	A38
Deacon Way SE17	A63
Dean Bradley St. SW1	A61
Dean Farrar St. SW1	A60
Dean Ryle St. SW1	A61
Dean St.	**20**
Dean St. W1	B40
Dean Stanley St. SW1	A61
Dean Trench St. SW1	A61
Deanery St. W1	A49
Deans Ct. EC4	B43

Deans Ms. W1	B39
Deans Pl. SW1	B60
Deans Yd. SW1	A60
Delamere Ter. W2	A36
Delancey St. NW1	A32
Delhi St. N1	A34
Delverton Rd. SE17	B63
Denbigh Pl. SW1	B60
Denbigh St. SW1	B60
Denman St.	**20**
Denman St. W1	A50
Denmark Gro. N1	A35
Denmark Pl. WC2	B40
Denmark St.	**20**
Denmark St. WC2	B40
Denning Clo. NW8	B30
Denny Cres. SE11	B62
Denny St. SE11	B62
Denyer St. SW3	B57
Derby Gro. W1	B51
Derby St. W1	B49
Dering St.	**18**
Dering St. W1	B39
Devonshire Clo. W1	A39
Devonshire Ms. S. W1	A39
Devonshire Ms. W. W1	A39
Devonshire Ms. W1	A39
Devonshire Pl. W1	A39
Devonshire Row EC2	B44
Devonshire Sq. EC2	B45
Devonshire St. W1	A39
Devonshire Ter. W2	B36
Dewey Rd. N1	A35
Dial Wk., The W8	B46
Diana Pl. NW1	A39
Dickens Sq. SE1	A63
Dignum St. N1	A35
Disney Pl. SE1	B53
Disney St. SE1	B53
Distaff La. EC4	A53
Distin St. SE11	B62
Distin St. SE11	B62
Dock St. E1	A55
Dodson St. SE1	A62
Dolben St. SE1	B53
Dolland St. SE11	B62
Dombey St. WC1	A41
Dominion St. EC2	A44
Donegal St. N1	A35
Donne Pl. SW3	A57
Doon St. SE1	B52

Doric Way NW1	B33
Dorrington St. EC1	A42
Dorset Clo. NW1	A38
Dorset Ms. SW1	A59
Dorset Pl. SW1	B60
Dorset Ri.	**25**
Dorset Ri. EC4	B42
Dorset Sq. NW1	A38
Dorset St. W1	A38
Doughty Ms. WC1	A41
Doughty St. WC1	A41
Douglas St. SW1	B60
Douro Pl. W8	B46
Dove Ms. SW5	B56
Dovehouse St. SW3	B57
Dover St.	**18**
Dover St. W1	A49
Dover Yd. W1	A49
Down St. W1	B49
Downgate Hill EC4	A54
Downing St.	**22**
Downing St. SW1	B51
Doyce St. SE1	B53
Doyley St. SW1	A58
Drake St. WC1	A41
Draycott Av. SW3	A57
Draycott Pl. SW3	B58
Draycott Ter. SW1	B58
Drayton Gdns. SW10	B56
Druid St. SE1	B55
Drum St. E1	B45
Drummond Cres. NW1	B33
Drummond Gate SW1	B60
Drummond St. NW1	B33
Drury La.	**21**
Drury La. WC2	B41
Dryden St. WC2	B41
Duchess Ms. W1	A39
Duchess St. W1	B39
Duchy St. SE1	A52
Duck La. W1	B40
Dudley St. W2	A37
Dudmaston Ms. SW3	B57
Dufferin St. EC1	A44
Dufours Pl. W1	B40
Duke of Wellington Pl. SW1	B49
Duke of York St. SW1	A50
Duke St. SW1	A50
Duke St. W1	B39
Duke Street Hill SE1	B54
Dukes Ms. W1	B39

Dukes Pl. EC3 — B45
Dukes Rd. WC1 — B33
Duncan St. N1 — A35
Duncannon St. WC2 — A51
Dunraven St. W1 —
Dunstable Ms. W1 — A39
Durham House St. WC2 — A51
Durham Pl. SW3 — B58
Dyott St. WC1 — B41
Dysart St. EC2 — A44

Eagle Ct. EC1 — A43
Eagle Pl. SW1 — A50
Eagle St. WC1 — B41
Eamont St. NW8 — A30
Earl St. EC2 — A44
Earlham St. — **20**
Earlham St. WC2 — B41
Earnshaw St. WC2 — B41
Easleys Ms. W1 — B39
East Harding St. EC4 — B42
East Poultry Av. EC1 — A43
East Smithfield E1 — A55
East St. EC2 — B44
East St. SE17 — B63
East Tenter St. E1 — B45
Eastbourne Ms. W2 — B36
Eastbourne Ter. W2 — B36
Eastcastle St. W1 — B40
Eastcheap EC3 — A54
Easton St. WC1 — B35
Eaton Clo. SW1 — B58
Eaton Gate SW1 — A58
Eaton La. SW1 — A59
Eaton Ms. N. SW1 — A58
Eaton Ms. S. SW1 — A59
Eaton Ms. W. SW1 — A59
Eaton Pl. SW1 — A58
Eaton Row SW1 — A59
Eaton Sq. SW1 — A58
Eaton Ter. SW1 — A58
Eaton Terrace Ms. SW1 — A58
Ebor St. E1 — A45
Ebury Bri. SW1 — B59
Ebury Bridge Est. SW1 — B59
Ebury Bridge Rd. SW1 — B59
Ebury Ms. E. SW1 — A59
Ebury Ms. SW1 — A59
Ebury Sq. SW1 — B59
Ebury St. SW1 — B59
Eccleston Bri. SW1 — A59

Eccleston Ms. SW1 — A59
Eccleston Pl. SW1 — B59
Eccleston Sq. SW1 — B59
Eccleston Square Ms. SW1 — B59
Eccleston St. SW1 — A59
Eckersley St. E1 — A45
Eckford St. N1 — A35
Edgware Rd. NW8 — A37
Edinburgh Gate SW1 — B48
Edward Ms. NW1 — B32
Edward Sq. N1 — A34
Edwards Ms. W1 — B39
Egerton Cres. SW3 — A57
Egerton Crescent Pl. SW3 — A57
Egerton Gardens Ms. SW3 — A57
Egerton Gdns. SW3 — A57
Egerton Pl. SW3 — A57
Egerton Ter. SW3 — A57
Elba Pl. SE17 — B63
Elder St. E1 — A45
Eldon Rd. W8 — A56
Eldon St. EC2 — B44
Elephant & Castle SE1 — B63
Elephant Rd. SE17 — B63
Elizabeth St. SW1 — A59
Elliots Row SE11 — B63
Ellis St. SW1 — A58
Elm Park Gdns. SW7 — B57
Elm Park La. SW3 — B56
Elm Pl. SW7 — B57
Elm St. WC1 — A42
Elm Tree Clo. NW8 — B30
Elm Tree Rd. NW8 — B30
Elms Ms. W2 — A47
Elnathan Ms. W9 — A36
Elvaston Ms. SW7 — A56
Elvaston Pl. SW7 — A56
Elverton St. SW1 — B60
Ely Pl. EC1 — B42
Elystan Pl. SW3 — B57
Elystan St. SW3 — B57
Elystan Wk. NW1 — A35
Embankment Pl. WC2 — A51
Emerald St. WC1 — A41
Emerson St. SE1 — A53
Emery Hill St. SW1 — A60
Emperors Gate SW7 — A56
Endell St. — **21**
Endell St. WC2 — B41

Endsleigh Gdns. WC1 — B33
Endsleigh Pl. WC1 — A40
Endsleigh St. WC1 — B33
Enford St. W1 — A38
English Grn. SE1 — B54
English Grounds SE1 — A53
Ennismore Gardens Ms. SW7 — A57
Ennismore Gdns. SW7 — B47
Ennismore Ms. SW7 — B47
Ennismore St. SW7 — A57
Ensor Ms. SW7 — B56
Epworth St. EC2 — A44
Erasmus St. SW1 — B60
Errol St. EC1 — A44
Essex Ct. EC4 — B42
Essex St. — **24**
Essex St. WC2 — B42
Esterbrooke St. SW1 — B60
Ethel St. SE17 — B63
Euston Gro. NW1 — B33
Euston Rd. NW1 — A39
Euston Sq. NW1 — B33
Euston St. NW1 — B33
Euston Station Colonnade NW1 — B33
Evelyn Gdns. SW7 — B56
Evelyn Yd. W1 — B40
Evershott St. NW1 — A33
Everton Bldgs. NW1 — B33
Ewer St. SE1 — B53
Exchange Arc. EC2 — A45
Exeter St. WC2 — A51
Exhibition Rd. SW7 — B47
Exmouth Mkt. EC1 — A42
Exton St. SE1 — B52
Eyre Ct. NW8 — A30
Eyre Street Hill EC1 — A42
Fair St. SE1 — B55
Fairbolt St. SW7 — A57
Fairchild St. EC2 — A45
Fairlop Pl. NW8 — B30
Falcon Clo. SE1 — A53
Falcon Clo. SE1 — B53
Falconberg Ms. W1 — B40
Falmouth Rd. SE1 — A63
Fann St. EC1 — A43
Farm St. W1 — A49
Farnham Pl. SE1 — B53
Farringdon Rd. EC1 — A42
Farringdon Rd. EC1 — B35
Farringdon St. — **25**

Farringdon St. EC1	B42
Fashion St. E1	B45
Featherstone St. EC1	A44
Fenchurch Av. EC3	A54
Fenchurch Bldgs. EC3	B45
Fenchurch Pl. EC3	A54
Fenchurch St. EC3	A54
Fenning St. SE1	B54
Fernsby St. WC1	B35
Fetter La.	**25**
Fetter La. EC4	B42
Field Ct. WC1	A42
Field Pl. EC1	B35
Fife Ter. N1	A35
Finch La. EC3	B44
Finchley Pl. NW8	A30
Finchley Rd. NW8	A30
Finck St. SE1	B52
Finsbury Av. EC2	B44
Finsbury Cir. EC2	B44
Finsbury Mkt. EC2	A44
Finsbury Pavement EC2	A44
Finsbury Sq. EC2	A44
Finsbury St. EC2	A44
First St. SW3	A57
Fish Street Hill EC3	A54
Fisher Sq. WC1	B41
Fisher Street Est. NW8	A37
Fisherton St. NW8	A37
Fitzalan St. SE11	B62
Fitzhardinge St. W1	B38
Fitzmaurice Pl. W1	A49
Fitzroy Ms. W1	A40
Fitzroy Sq. W1	A40
Fitzroy St. W1	A40
Flank St. E1	A55
Flaxman Ter. WC1	B34
Fleet La. EC4	B43
Fleet Sq. WC1	B35
Fleet St.	**25**
Fleet St. WC2	B42
Fleet Street Hill E1	A45
Fleur de Lis St. E1	A45
Flitcroft St. WC2	B40
Flood St. SW3	B57
Floral St. WC2	A51
Flower & Dean St. E1	B45
Foley St. W1	A40
Folgate St. E1	A45
Fore St. EC2	B44
Fore Street Av. EC2	B44

Formosa St. W9	A36
Forset St. W1	B38
Fort St. E1	B45
Fortune St. EC1	A43
Fosbury Ms. W2	A46
Foster La. EC2	B43
Fouberts Pl. W1	B40
Foulis St. W1	B57
Fountain Ct. EC4	A52
Fournier St. E1	A45
Fox Ct. EC1	A42
Frampton St. NW8	A37
Francis St. W1	A60
Franklins Row SW3	B58
Frazier St. SE1	B52
Frederick Clo. W2	B38
Frederick St. WC1	B34
Friar St. EC4	B43
Friday St. EC4	A53
Frith St.	**20**
Frith St. W1	B40
Frying Pan Alley E1	B45
Fulham Rd. SW3	B56
Fulton Ms. W2	A46
Fulwood Pl. WC1	B42
Furnival St.	**25**
Furnival St. EC4	B42
Fynes St. SW1	A60
Gage St. WC1	A41
Gainsford St. SE1	B55
Galen Pl. WC1	B41
Gambia St. SE1	B53
Ganton St. W1	B40
Garbutt Pl. W1	A39
Garden Rd. NW8	B30
Garden Row SE1	B63
Garden Ter. SW1	B60
Gardners La. EC4	A53
Garlick Hill EC4	A53
Garnault Ms. EC1	B35
Garnault Pl. EC1	B35
Garrett St. EC1	A43
Garrick St.	**21**
Garrick St. WC2	A51
Gaspar Ms. SW5	A56
Gate St. WC2	B41
Gateforth St. NW8	A37
Gateways, The SW3	B58
Gatliff Rd. SW1	B59
Gaunt St. SE1	A63
Gayfere St. SW1	A61
Gaywood St. SE1	A63

Gee St. EC1	A43
Gees Ct. W1	B39
George Inn Yd. SE1	B54
George Row SE16	B55
George St. W1	B38
George Yd. W1	A49
Gerald Rd. SW1	B59
Gerrard St. W1	A50
Gerridge St. SE1	A62
Ghenies Ms. WC1	A40
Gibson Rd. SE11	B62
Gilbert Pl. WC1	B41
Gilbert Rd. SE11	B62
Gilbert St. W1	B39
Gildea St. W1	A39
Giles Cir. WC1	B40
Gillingham Ms. SW1	A59
Gillingham Row SW1	B59
Gillingham St. SW1	B59
Gilston Rd. SW10	B56
Giltspur St. EC1	B43
Gladstone St. SE1	A62
Glasgow Ter. SW1	B59
Glasshill St. SE1	B53
Glasshouse St.	**19**
Glasshouse St. W1	A50
Glasshouse Wk. SE11	B61
Glasshouse Yd. EC1	A43
Gledhow Gdns. SW5	B56
Glendower Pl. SW7	A57
Glentworth St. NW1	A38
Globe St. SE1	A63
Gloucester Av. NW1	A32
Gloucester Cres. NW1	A32
Gloucester Gate Ms. NW1	A32
Gloucester Gate NW1	A32
Gloucester Gdns. W2	B36
Gloucester Ms. W. W2	B36
Gloucester Ms. W2	B36
Gloucester Pl. NW1	A38
Gloucester Pl. W1	A38
Gloucester Pl. W1	B38
Gloucester Rd. SW7	A56
Gloucester Sq. W2	B37
Gloucester St. SW1	B59
Gloucester Ter. W2	B36
Gloucester Way EC1	B35
Glynde Ms. SW3	A58
Godfrey St. SW3	B57
Godliman St. EC4	B43
Godson St. N1	A35

oodwin Ct. NW1	A33	Grays Inn Pl. WC1	A42	Great Tichfield St.	19
Golden La. EC1	A43	Grays Inn Rd. WC1	A42	Great Tichfield St. W1	A39
Golden Lane Est. EC1	A43	Grays Inn Rd. W1	B34	Great Tower St. EC3	A54
Golden Sq.	**19**	Grays Inn Rd. WC1	A42	Great Turnstile WC2	B42
Golden Sq. W1	A50	Great Castle St.	B39	Great Winchester St.	B44
Goldford Pl. NW1	A37	Great Central St.	A38	EC2	
oldington Cres.	A33	NW1		**Greek St.**	**20**
NW1		Great Chapel St. W1	B40	Greek St. W1	B40
Goldington St. NW1	A33	Great College St. SW1	A61	Green Dragon Yd. E1	B45
oldman Clo. E2	A45	Great Cumberland Ms.	B38	Green St. W1	A48
Goodge Pl. W1	A40	W1		Green Ter. EC1	B35
Goodge St. W1	B40	Great Cumberland Pl.	B38	Greenberry St. NW8	A30
Goodman St. E1	A55	W1		Greencoat Pl. SW1	A60
Goodmans Yd. E1	A55	Great Dover St. SE1	B53	Greencoat Row SW1	A60
oods Way NW1	A34	Great Eastern St. EC2	A44	Greenham Clo. SE1	A62
Goodwins Ct. WC2	A51	Great Eastern Wk.	B45	Greenhills Rents EC1	A43
Goose Yd. EC1	B35	EC2		Greenwell St. W1	A39
Gordon Sq. WC1	A40	Great George St. SW1	B50	Greet St. SE1	B52
Gordon St. WC1	A33	Great Guildford St.	B53	Grenville Pl. SW7	A56
ore St. SW7	A56	SE1		Grenville St. WC1	A41
Goring St. EC3	B45	Great James St. WC1	A41	Gresham St. EC2	B43
osfield St. W1	A39	**Great Marlborough St.**	**19**	Gresse St. W1	B40
Goslett Yd. WC2	B40	Great Marlborough St.	B40	Greville St. EC1	B42
Goswell Rd. EC1	B35	W1		Grey Eagle St. E1	A45
Gough Sq.	**25**	Great Maze Pond SE1	B53	Greycoat Pl. SW1	A60
Gough Sq. EC4	B42	Great New St. EC4	B42	Greycoat St. SW1	A60
Gough St. WC1	A42	**Great Newport St.**	**20**	Grimsby St. E2	A45
Goulston St. E1	B45	Great Newport St.	A51	Grindal St. SE1	B52
Gower Ct. WC1	A40	WC2		Groom Pl. SW1	A59
Gower Ms. WC1	A40	Great Ormond St.	A41	Grosvenor Cres. SW1	B48
Gower Pl. WC1	A40	WC1		Grosvenor Crescent	B48
Gower St. WC1	A40	Great Percy St. WC1	B35	Ms. SW1	
Gracechurch St. EC3	A54	Great Peter St. SW1	A60	Grosvenor Est. SW1	A60
Grafton Ms. W1	A40	**Great Portland St.**	**19**	Grosvenor Gardens	A59
Grafton Pl. NW1	B33	Great Portland St.	A39	Ms. N. SW1	
Grafton St.	**18**	W1		Grosvenor Gate W1	A48
Grafton St. W1	A49	Great Pulteney St.	B40	Grosvenor Gdns. SW1	A59
Grafton Way W1	A40	W1		Grosvenor Hill W1	A49
Graham Ter. SW3	B58	**Great Queen St.**	**21**	Grosvenor Pl. SW1	B49
Granary Way NW1	A33	Great Queen St. WC2	B41	**Grosvenor Sq.**	**18**
Granby St. E2	A45	**Great Russell St.**	**20**	Grosvenor Sq. W1	A49
Granby Ter. NW1	B33	Great Russell St. WC1	A40	**Grosvenor St.**	**18**
Grand Av. EC1	A43	**Great Scotland Yd.**	**23**	Grosvenor St. W1	A49
Grange Ct. WC2	B42	Great Scotland Yd.	B51	Grove End Rd. NW8	B30
Grant St. N1	A35	SW1		Grove Gdns. NW8	B30
Grantham Pl. W1	B49	Great Smith St. SW1	A60	Guildhall Bldgs. EC2	B44
Granville Pl. W1	B38	Great St. Helens EC3	B44	Guildhall Yd. EC2	B44
Granville Sq. WC1	B35	Great St. Thomas	A53	Guildhouse St. SW1	B59
Granville St. WC1	B35	Apostle EC4		Guilford Pl. WC1	A41
Grape St. WC2	B41	Great Suffolk St. SE1	B53	Guilford St. WC1	A41
Gravel La. E1	B45	Great Sutton St. EC1	A43	Guinness Bldgs. SE11	B63
Gray St. SE1	B52	Great Swan Alley EC2	B44	Guinness Bldgs. SW3	B58

Gundulf St. SE11	B62	Harp Alley EC4	B42	Henrietta St. WC2	A51
Gunthorpe St. E1	B45	Harp La. EC3	A54	Hensridge Pl. NW8	A30
Gutter La. EC2	B43	Harper Rd. SE1	A63	Heralds Ct. SE11	B62
Guy St. SE1	B54	Harpur St. WC1	A41	Herbal Hill EC1	A42
Gwynne Pl. WC1	B35	Harriet St. SW1	B48	Herbert Cres. SW1	A58
Habet Rd. W2	A37	Harriet Wk. SW1	B48	Herbrand St. WC1	A41
Half Moon Pass. E1	B45	Harrington Gdns. SW7	B56	Hercules Rd. SE1	A62
Half Moon St. W1	A49	Harrington Rd. SW7	A56	Hereford Sq. SW7	B56
Halkin Arc. SW1	A58	Harrington Sq. NW1	A33	Hermes St. N1	A35
Halkin Pl. SW1	A58	Harrington St. NW1	B33	Hermitage St. W2	A37
Halkin St. SW1	A58	Harrison St. WC1	B34	Herrick St. SW1	B60
Hall Gate NW8	B30	Harrow Pl. E1	B45	Hertford Pl. W1	A40
Hall Pl. W2	A37	Harrowby St. W1	B38	Hertford St. W1	B49
Hallam St. W1	A39	Hart St. EC3	A55	Hesper Ms. SW5	B56
Hallfield Est. W2	B36	Harwich La. EC2	A45	Hewett St. EC2	A44
Halsey St. SW3	A58	Hasker St. SW3	A58	Heygate St. SE17	B63
Hamilton Pl. W1	B49	Hastings St. WC1	B34	Hide Pl. SW1	B60
Hamilton Sq. SE1	B54	Hatfield St. SE1	A52	High Holborn	21
Hampden Clo. NW1	A33	Hatherley Gro. W2	B36	High Holborn WC1	B41
Hampden Gurney Pl. W1	B38	Hatherley St. SW1	B60	High Timber St. EC4	A53
Hampstead Rd. NW1	A33	Hatton Gdn. EC1	A42	Hill St.	18
Hampton St. SE17	B63	Hatton Pl. EC1	A42	Hill St. W1	A49
Hanbury St. E1	A45	Hatton Row NW8	A37	Hills Pl. W1	B40
Hand Ct. WC1	B42	Hatton St. NW8	A37	Hind Ct.	28
Handel St. WC1	A41	Hatton Wall EC1	A42	Hind Ct. EC4	B42
Hankey Pl. SE1	B54	Haunch of Venison Yd. W1	B39	Hinde St. W1	B39
Hanover Gate Mans. NW1	N31	Havelock St. N1	A34	Hobart Pl. SW1	A58
Hanover Gate NW1	B31	Hay Hill W1	A49	Holbein Ms. SW3	A58
Hanover Ms. NW1	B31	Haydon St. EC3	A55	Holbein Pl. SW1	B58
Hanover Sq.	18	Hayes Pl. NW1	A38	Holborn Cir. EC1	B42
Hanover Sq. W1	B39	Hayles St. SE11	B63	Holborn Viaduct	28
Hanover Ter. NW1	B31	Haymarket	22	Holborn Viaduct EC1	B42
Hans Cres. SW1	B48	Haymarket SW1	A50	Holborn WC1	B41
Hans Pl. SW1	A58	Hayne St. EC1	A43	Holford St. WC1	B35
Hans Rd. SW3	A58	Hays La. SE1	B54	Holland St. SE1	A53
Hans St. SW1	A58	Hays Ms. W1	A49	Hollen St. W1	B40
Hanson St. W1	A40	Haywards Pl. EC1	A43	Holles St.	18
Hanway Pl. W1	B40	Headfort Pl. SW1	B49	Holles St. W1	B39
Hanway St. W1	B40	Hearn St. EC2	A44	Holyoake Rd. SE11	B63
Harcourt St. W1	A38	Heathcote St. WC1	B34	Holyrood St. SE1	B54
Harcourt Ter. SW10	B56	Heddon St. W1	A50	Holywell La. EC2	A44
Hardwick St. EC1	B35	Helmet Row EC1	A43	Holywell Row EC2	A44
Hardwidge St. SE1	B54	Hemingford Rd. N1	A35	Homer Row W1	A37
Hare Pl. EC4	B42	Hemus Pl. SW3	B57	Homer St. W1	A38
Harewood Av. NW1	A33	Henderson Dr. NW8	B30	Honduras St. EC1	A43
Harewood Pl. W1	B39	Heneage La. EC3	B45	Honey La. EC2	B43
Harewood Row NW1	A38	Heneage St. E1	B45	Hooper St. E1	A55
Harley Gdns. SW10	B56	Henrietta Ms. WC1	B34	Hoopers Ct. SW3	B48
Harley Pl. W1	B39	Henrietta Pl.	18	Hopetown St. E1	B45
Harley St. W1	A39	Henrietta Pl. W1	B39	Hopkins St. W1	B40
		Henrietta St.	21	Hopton St. SE1	A53
				Hornbeam Clo. SE11	A63

Horse Guards Av.	23	Inverness Ms. W2	B36	Kendall Pl. W1	B38
Horse Guards Av. SW1	B51	Inverness Pl. W2	A46	Kendall St. W2	B37
		Inverness Ter. W2	B36	Kendrick Ms. SW7	A57
Horse Guards Rd.	23	Ireland Yd. EC4	B43	Kennings Way SE11	B62
Horse Guards Rd. SW1	B50	Ironmonger La. EC2	B44	Kennington La. SE11	B62
		Irving St.	20	Kennington Rd. SE1	A62
Horseferry Rd. SW1	A60	Irving St. WC2	A50	Kenrick Pl. W1	A38
Horsleydown La. SE1	B55	Isabella St. SE1	B52	Kensington Court Pl. W8	A56
Hosier La. EC1	B43	Islington High St. N1	A35		
Hotspur St. SE11	B62	Ives St. SW3	B57	Kensington Ct. W8	B46
Houghton St. WC2	B41	Ixworth Pl. SW3	A57	Kensington Gardens Sq. W2	B36
Houndsditch EC3	B44	Jacobs Well Pl. W1	B39		
Howell Wk. SE17	B63	**James St.**	21	Kensington Gate W8	A56
Howick Pl. SW1	A60	James St. W1	B39	Kensington Gore SW7	B46
Howland Ms. E. W1	A40	James St. WC2	B41	Kensington Palace Gdns. W8	B46
Howland Ms. W. W1	A40	Jay Ms. SW7	B46		
Howland St. W1	A40	**Jermyn St.**	19	Kensington Rd. W8	B46
Howley Pl. W2	A36	Jermyn St. SW1	B50	Kensington Sq. W8	B46
Hudson Pl. SW1	A59	Jeroma Cres. NW8	B30	Kent Pass. NW1	B31
Huggin Hill EC4	B53	Jerome St. E1	A45	Kent Ter. NW1	B31
Hugh Ms. SW1	B59	Jerusalem Pass. EC1	B43	Kenton St. WC1	B34
Hugh St. SW1	B59	Jewry St. EC3	B45	Keppel Row SE1	B53
Hungerford Bri.	23	Joan St. SE1	B52	Keppel St. WC1	A40
Hungerford Bri. WC2	A51	Jockeys Fields WC1	A42	Kerbela St. E2	A45
Hunter St. WC1	B34	Johanna St. SE1	B52	Keyston Cres. N1	A34
Huntley St. WC1	A40	**John Adam St.**	23	Keyworth St. SE1	A63
Hunton St. E1	A45	John Adam St. WC2	A51	Kiffen St. EC2	A44
Huntsworth Ms. NW1	A38	John Aird Ct.	A36	Killick St. N1	A34
Hyde Park Corner W1	B49	**John Carpenter St.**	25	King & Queen St. SE17	B63
Hyde Park Cres. W2	B37	John Carpenter St. EC4	A52		
Hyde Park Gate Ms. SW7	B46	John Felton Rd. SE16	B55	King Charles St. SW1	B51
		John Fisher St. E1	A55	King Edward St. EC1	B43
Hyde Park Gate SW7	B46	John Islip St. SW1	B60	King Edward Wk. SE1	A62
Hyde Park Gdns. Ms. W2	B37	**John Princes St.**	18	King James St. SE1	A63
		John Princes St. W1	B39	King John Ct. EC2	A45
Hyde Park Gdns. W2	A47	John St. WC1	A42	**King St.**	21
Hyde Park Gdns. W2	B37	Johns Ms. WC1	A42	King St. EC2	B44
Hyde Park Mans. NW1	A37	Johnsons Pl. SW1	B60	King St. SW1	B50
Hyde Park Pl. W2	B38	Joiner St. SE1	B54	King St. WC2	A51
Hyde Park Sq. W2	B37	Jonathan St. SE11	B61	King William St. EC4	B44
Hyde Park St. W2	B37	Jones St. W1	A49	Kinghorn St. EC1	B43
Idol La. EC3	A54	Jubileee Pl. SW3	B57	Kingly Ct. W1	A50
Iliffe St. SE17	B63	Judd St. WC1	B34	**Kingly St.**	19
Iliffe Yd. SE17	B63	Junction Ms. W2	B37	Kingly St. W1	B40
Imperial Institute Rd. SW7	A56	Juxon St. SE11	A62	Kings Arms Yd. EC2	B44
		Kean St. WC2	B41	Kings Bench St. SE1	B53
India St. EC3	A55	Keeley St. WC2	B41	Kings Bench Wk. EC4	A52
Ingestre Pl. W1	B40	Kell St. SE1	A63	Kings Cross Rd. WC1	B34
Inglebert St. EC1	B35	Kelso Pl. W8	A56	Kings Head Yd. SE1	B54
Ingram Clo. SE1	A62	**Kemble St.**	21	Kings Ms. WC1	A42
Inner Circle NW1	B31	Kemble St. WC2	B41	Kings Pl. SE1	A63
Insurance St. WC1	B35			Kings Rd. SW1	A58

83

Kings Scholars Pass. SW1	A60	Langdon Pl. SW1	A58	Leonards Ter. SW3	B58		
Kings Ter. NW1	A33	Langford Ct. NW8	A30	Leveret St. SW3	B57		
Kingscote St. EC4	A53	Langford Pl. NW8	A30	Lewis Trust Bldgs. SW3	B57		
Kingsley Ms. W8	A56	Langham Pl. W1	B39				
Kingsmill Ter. NW8	A30	Langham St. W1	B39	Lewisham St. SW1	B50		
Kingsway	**21**	Langley St. WC2	B41	Lexham Gdns. W8	A56		
Kingsway WC2	B41	Langton Clo. WC1	B35	Lexham Wk. W8	A56		
Kinnerton Pl. N. SW1	B48	Lansdowne Row W1	A49	**Lexington St.**	**19**		
Kinnerton Pl. S. SW1	B48	Lansdowne Ter. WC1	A41	Lexington St. W1	B40		
Kinnerton St. SW1	B48	Lant St. SE1	B53	Leyden St. E1	B45		
Kipling Est. SE1	B54	Larcom St. SE17	B63	Library St. SE1	A63		
Kipling St. SE1	B54	Laud St. SE11	B61	Ligonier St. E2	A45		
Kirby Gro. SE1	B54	Launcelot St. SE1	B52	Lilac Pl. SE11	B61		
Kirby St. EC1	A42	Launceston Pl. W8	A56	Lilestone Est. NW8	A37		
Knightrider St. EC4	A53	Laverton Pl. SW5	B56	Lilestone St. NW8	A37		
Knights Wk. SE11	B62	Lavina Gro. N1	A34	Lillington Gardens Est. SW1	B60		
Knightsbridge Clo. SW1	B48	Lavington St. SE1	B53				
Knightsbridge SW7	B47	Lawrence La. EC2	B43	Lime St. EC3	A54		
Knox St. W1	A38	Lawrence Pountney Hill EC4	A54	Lincoln St. SW3	B58		
Kynance Ms. SW7	A56			**Lincolns Inn Fields**	**24**		
Kynance Pl. SW7	A56	Lawrence Pountney La. EC4	A54	Lincolns Inn Fields WC2	B41		
Lackington St. EC2	A44						
Lafone St. SE1	B55	Lawrence St. NW1	A34	Lindsey St. EC1	A42		
Lamb St. E1	A45	Laxton Pl. NW1	B32	Linhope St. NW1	A38		
Lambeth High St. SE1	B61	Laystall St. EC1	A42	Liplington Pl. NW1	A33		
Lambeth Ms. SE11	B61	Layton Rd. N1	A35	**Lisle St.**	**20**		
Lambeth Palace Rd. SE1	A61	Leadenhall Pl. EC3	B44	Lisle St. WC2	A50		
		Leadenhall St. EC3	B44	Lisson Gro. NW8	B30		
Lambeth Rd. SE1	A61	Leake Ct. SE1	B52	Lisson St. NW1	A37		
Lambeth St. E1	B45	Leake St. SE1	B52	Litchfield St. WC2	B41		
Lambeth Wk. SE11	B61	Leather La. EC1	A42	Little Albany St. NW1	B32		
Lambs Bldgs. EC1	A44	Leathermarket St. SE1	B54	Little Argyll St. W1	B40		
Lambs Conduit Pass. WC1	A41	Lecky St. SW7	B57	Little Boltons, The SW10	B56		
		Leeke St. WC1	B34				
Lambs Conduit St. WC1	A41	Lees Pl. W1	A48	Little Britain EC1	B43		
		Leicester Ct. WC2	A50	Little Chester St. SW1	A59		
Lambs Pass. EC1	A44	**Leicester Sq.**	**20**	Little College St. SW1	A61		
Lamlash St. SE11	A63	Leicester Sq. WC2	A50	Little Dorrit Ct. SE1	B53		
Lanark Pl. W9	A36	Leicester St. WC2	A50	Little Edward St. NW1	B32		
Lancaster Ct. W2	A46	Leigh Hunt St. SE1	B53	Little George St. SW1	B51		
Lancaster Gate W2	A46	Leigh St. WC1	B34	Little Marlborough St. W1	B40		
Lancaster Ms. W2	B36	Leinster Gdns. W2	B36				
Lancaster Pl.	23	Leinster Ms. W2	A46	Little New St. EC4	B42		
Lancaster Pl. WC2	A51	Leinster Pl. W2	B36	Little Newport St. WC2	A50		
Lancaster St. SE1	A53	Leinster Ter. W2	A46				
Lancaster Ter. W2	A47	Leman St. E2	B45	Little Portland St. N1	B39		
Lancelot Pl. SW7	B48	Lennox Gardens Ms. SW1	A58	Little Russell St. WC1	B41		
Lancing St,. NW1	B32			Little Smith St. SW1	A60		
Landon Pl. SW1	A58	Lennox Gdns. SW1	A58	Little Somerset St. E1	B45		
Lanfranc St. SE1	A62	Lenthall Pl. SW7	A56	Little St. James St. SW1	B50		
		Leo Yd. EC1	A43				
		Leonard St. EC2	A44	Little Tichfield St. W1	B39		

Little Trinity La. EC4 — A53
Little Turnstile St. WC2 — B41
Liverpool Rd. N1 — A35
Liverpool St. EC2 — B44
Livonia St. W1 — B40
Lloyd Baker St. WC1 — B35
Lloyd Sq. WC1 — B35
Lloyd St. WC1 — B35
Lloyds Av. EC3 — B44
Lloyds Row EC1 — B35
Lockyer St. SE1 — B54
Lodge Rd. NW8 — B30
Lolesworth Clo. — B45
Lolesworth St. E1 — B45
Lollard Pl. SE11 — B62
Lollard St. SE11 — B62
Loman St. SE1 — B53
Lombard La. EC4 — B42
Lombard St. EC3 — B44
London Bridge St. SE1 — B54
London Ms. W2 — B37
London Rd. SE1 — A63
London St. EC3 — A55
London St. W2 — B37
London Wall EC2 — B43
Long Acre — 21
Long Acre WC2 — A51
Long La. EC1 — A43
Long La. SE1 — B54
Long Yd. WC1 — A41
Longford St. NW1 — B32
Longmore St. SW1 — B60
Longville Rd. SE11 — B63
Lord Hills Rd. W2 — A36
Lord North St. SW1 — A61
Lorenzo St. WC1 — B34
Lorne Clo. NW1 — B31
Lothbury EC2 — B44
Loughborough St. SE11 — B62
Loundoun Rd. NW8 — A30
Lovat La. EC3 — A54
Love La. EC2 — A43
Lower Belgrave St. SW1 — A59
Lower Grosvenor Pl. SW1 — A59
Lower James St. W1 — A50
Lower John St. W1 — A50
Lower Marsh SE1 — B52

Lower Newport St. WC2 — A50
Lower Sloane St. SW11 — B58
Lower Thames St. EC3 — A54
Lowndes Clo. SW1 — A58
Lowndes Pl. SW1 — A58
Lowndes Sq. SW1 — B48
Lowndes St. SW1 — A58
Loxham St. WC1 — B34
Lucan Pl. SW3 — B57
Ludgate Cir. — 25
Ludgate Cir. EC4 — B43
Ludgate Hill — 25
Ludgate Hill EC4 — B43
Ludgate Sq. EC4 — B43
Luke St. EC2 — A44
Lumley St. W1 — B39
Lupus St. SW1 — B59
Luton St. NW8 — A37
Luxborough St. W1 — A38
Lyall Ms. E. SW1 — A58
Lyall Ms. W. SW1 — A58
Lyall St. SW1 — A58
Lygon Pl. SW1 — A59
Lyons Pl. NW8 — A37
Mabledon Pl. WC1 — B34
Macclesfield Bri. NW8 — A31
Macclesfield St. W1 — A50
Macfarren Pl. NW1 — A39
Mackennal St. NW8 — A30
Macklin St. WC2 — A51
Mackworth St. NW1 — B33
Macquire St. E1 — B55
Maddox St. — 18
Maddox St. W1 — A49
Magdalen St. SE1 — B54
Magpie Alley EC4 — B42
Maguire St. E1 — B55
Maida Av. W2 — A36
Maiden La. — 21
Maiden La. WC2 — A51
Maidstone Bldgs. SE1 — B53
Makins St. SW3 — B57
Malet Pl. WC1 — A40
Malet St. WC1 — A40
Mall, The — 22
Mall, The SW1 — B50
Mallory St. NW8 — A37
Mallow St. EC1 — A44
Maltravers St. WC2 — A52

Malvern Ct. SW7 — A57
Manchester Sq. W1 — B38
Manchester St. W1 — A38
Mandela St. NW1 — A33
Mandeville Houses N1 — A35
Mandeville Pl. W1 — B39
Manette St. W1 — B40
Manningtree St. E1 — B45
Manor Pl. SE17 — B63
Manresa Rd. SW3 — B57
Mansell St. E1 — B45
Mansfield Ms. W1 — A39
Mansfield St. W1 — A39
Mansion House St. EC2 — B44
Manson Ms. SW7 — B56
Manson Pl. SW7 — B56
Maple Pl. W1 — A40
Maple St. W1 — A40
Marble Arch W1 — B38
Marble Quay E1 — B55
Marchmont St. WC1 — B34
Margaret St. — 18
Margaret St. W1 — B39
Margery St. WC1 — B35
Mark La. EC3 — A55
Mark St. EC2 — A44
Market Ms. W1 — B49
Market Pl. W1 — B40
Markham Sq. SW3 — B58
Markham St. SW3 — B57
Marlborough Alley SE1 — A52
Marlborough Bldgs. SW3 — A57
Marlborough Clo. SE17 — B63
Marlborough Ct. W1 — B40
Marlborough Hill NW8 — A30
Marlborough Rd. SW1 — B50
Marlborough St. SW3 — B57
Marloes, The NW8 — A30
Marshall Gdns. SE1 — A63
Marshall St. W1 — B40
Marshalsea Rd. SE1 — B53
Marsham St. SW1 — A60
Mart St. WC2 — B41
Martin La. EC4 — A54
Martlett Ct. WC2 — B41
Mary Ter. NW1 — A32
Marylebone Cir. NW1 — A38

85

Marylebone High St. W1 — B39
Marylebone La. — 18
Marylebone La. W1 — B39
Marylebone Ms. W1 — B39
Marylebone Pass. W1 — B39
Marylebone Rd. NW1 — A38
Marylebone St. W1 — A39
Marylee Way SE11 — B62
Mason St. SW1 — A50
Masons Arms Ms. W1 — B39
Masons Av. EC2 — B44
Mathew Parker St. SW1 — A60
Matilda St. N1 — A35
Maunsel St. SW1 — A60
Mayfair Pl. W1 — A49
Maygood St. N1 — A35
Mays Ct. WC2 — A51
McAuley Clo. SE1 — A62
McCoid Way SE1 — A62
McLeods Ms. SW7 — A56
Mead Row SE1 — A62
Meadow Row SE1 — A63
Meard St. W1 — B40
Mecklenburgh Pl. WC1 — A41
Mecklenburgh Sq. WC1 — B34
Medburn St. NW1 — A33
Medcalf Pl. EC1 — B35
Medway St. SW1 — A60
Melbourne Pl. WC2 — B42
Melbury Ter. NW1 — A38
Melcombe Pl. NW1 — A38
Melcombe St. NW1 — A38
Melior St. SE1 — B54
Melton Ct. SW7 — B57
Melton St. NW1 — B33
Mepham St. SE1 — B52
Mercer St. WC2 — B41
Meredith St. EC1 — B35
Merlin St. WC1 — B35
Mermaid Ct. SE1 — B54
Merrick Sq. SE1 — A63
Mews St. SW1 — A59
Meymott St. SE1 — B52
Middle St. EC1 — A43
Middle Temple La. — 24
Middle Temple La. EC4 — B42
Middlesex St. E1 — B45

Middleton Pass. EC1 — B35
Midford Pl. W1 — A40
Midhope St. WC1 — B34
Midland Rd. NW1 — A34
Milborne Gro. SW10 — B56
Milcote St. SE1 — A63
Miles La. EC4 — A54
Miles Pl. NW1 — A37
Milford La. WC2 — A52
Milk St. EC2 — B43
Mill St. SE1 — B55
Mill St. W1 — B39
Millbank SW1 — A61
Miller St. NW1 — A33
Millmans St. WC1 — A41
Milner St. SW3 — A58
Milroy Wk. SE1 — A52
Milton Ct. EC2 — A44
Milton St. EC2 — A44
Mincing La. EC3 — A54
Minera Ms. SW1 — A58
Minories EC3 — B45
Mint St. SE1 — B53
Mitchell St. EC1 — A43
Mitre Ct. EC2 — B43
Mitre Rd. SE1 — B52
Mitre St. EC3 — B45
Model Bldgs. WC1 — B35
Molyneux St. W1 — B38
Monck St. SW1 — A60
Moncorvo Clo. — B47
Monkton St. SE11 — B62
Monkwell Sq. EC2 — B43
Monmouth St. — 20
Monmouth St. WC2 — B41
Montagu Ms. N. W1 — A38
Montagu Ms. S. W1 — B38
Montagu Ms. W. W1 — B38
Montagu Pl. W1 — B38
Montagu Sq. W1 — B38
Montagu St. W1 — B38
Montague Clo. SE1 — A54
Montague Pl. WC1 — A40
Montague St. WC1 — A41
Montford St. SE1 — B45
Montpelier Ms. SW7 — A58
Montpelier Pl. SW7 — A57
Montpelier Sq. SW7 — B47
Montpelier St. SW7 — B47
Montpelier Ter. SW7 — B47
Montpelier Wk. SW7 — B47
Montreal Pl. WC2 — A51

Montrose Ct. SW7 — B4
Montrose Pl. SW1 — B4
Monument St. EC3 — A5
Moon St. N1 — A3
Moor La. EC2 — A4
Moor La. EC2 — B4
Moor St. W1 — B4
Moore St. SW3 — A5
Moorfields EC2 — B4
Moorgate EC2 — B4
Morecambe St. SE17 — B6
Moreton Pl. SW1 — B6
Moreton St. SW1 — B6
Moreton Ter. SW1 — B6
Morgans La. SE1 — B5
Morley St. SE1 — A6
Mornington Cres. NW1 — A3
Mornington Pl. NW1 — A3
Mornington St. NW1 — A3
Mornington Ter. NW1 — A3
Morocco St. SE1 — B5
Morpeth Ter. SW1 — A6
Mortimer Mkt. WC1 — A4
Mortimer St. W1 — B3
Morton Pl. SE1 — A6
Morwell St. WC1 — B4
Moscow Pl. W2 — B3
Mossop St. SW3 — B5
Motcomb St. SW1 — A5
Mount Pleasant WC1 — A4
Mount Row W1 — A4
Mount St. — 1
Mount St. W1 — A4
Moxon St. W1 — A3
Mulready St. NW8 — A3
Mulvaney Way SE1 — B5
Munster Sq. NW1 — B3
Munton Rd. SE17 — B6
Muriel St. N1 — A3
Murphy St. SE1 — A6
Muscovy St. EC3 — A5
Museum St. WC1 — B4
Myddleton Pass. EC1 — B3
Myddleton Sq. EC1 — B3
Myddleton St. EC1 — B3
Mylne St. EC1 — B3
Nash St. NW1 — B3
Nassau St. W1 — B4
Neal St. — 2
Neal St. WC2 — B4
Neathouse Clo. SW1 — A5

86

Nelson Sq. SE1	B53	Newman St. W1	B40	Nutford Pl. W1	B38
Netley St. NW1	B33	Newman Yd. W1	B40	O'Meara St. SE1	B53
Neville Clo. WC1	A34	Newmans Row WC2	B42	Oak Tree Rd. NW8	B30
Neville St. SW7	B57	Newnham St. E1	B45	Oakden St. SE11	B62
Neville Ter. SW7	B57	Newnham Ter. SE1	A62	Oakley La. E1	A62
New Bond St.	18	Newport Ct. WC2	A50	Oakley Sq. NW1	A33
New Bond St. W1	B39	Newport Pl. WC2	A50	Oat La. EC2	B43
New Bridge St.	25	Newport St. SE11	B61	Occupation Rd. SE17	B63
New Bridge St. EC4	B43	Newport St. WC2	A50	Octagon Arc. EC2	B44
New Broad St. EC2	A44	Newton St. WC2	B41	Ogle St. W1	A40
New Burlington Pl. W1	A50	Nicholas La. EC4	A50	Old Bailey EC4	B43
New Burlington St.	19	Nicolson St. SE1	B53	Old Barrack Yd. SW1	B48
New Burlington St. W1	A50	Noble St. EC2	B43	Old Bond St.	19
New Cavendish St. W1	B39	Noel St. W1	B40	Old Bond St. W1	A50
New Change EC4	B43	Norfolk Cres. W2	B37	Old Broad St. EC2	A44
New Compton St.	20	Norfolk Pl. W2	B37	Old Burlington St. W1	A49
New Compton St. WC2	A50	Norfolk Rd. NW8	A30	Old Castle St. E1	B45
New Coventry St. W1	A50	Norfolk Row SE11	A61	Old Cavendish St.	18
New Ct. WC2	B42	Norfolk Sq. W2	B37	Old Cavendish St. W1	B39
New Fetter La. EC4	B43	Norris St. SW1	A50	Old Change Ct. EC4	A53
New Goulston St. E1	B45	North Audley St. W1	B38	Old Church St. SW3	B57
New Inn St. EC2	A45	North Bank NW8	B30	Old Compton St.	20
New Inn Yd. EC2	A45	North Cres. W1	A40	Old Compton St. W1	B40
New Kent Rd. SE1	A63	North Ct. W1	A40	Old Gloucester St. WC1	A41
New North Pl. EC2	A45	North Gower St. NW1	B33		
New North St. WC1	A41	North Ms. WC1	A42	Old Jewry EC2	B44
New Oxford St.	20	North Ride W2	A47	Old Marylebone Rd. NW1	B37
New Oxford St. WC1	B40	North Row W1	B38	Old Montague St. E1	B45
New Palace Yd. SW1	B51	North Tenter St. E1	B45	Old Nichol St. E2	A45
New Quebec St. W1	B38	North Ter. SW3	A57	Old North St. WC1	A41
New Row WC2	A51	North Wharf Rd. W2	A37	Old Palace Yd. SW1	B51
New Sq. WC2	B42	Northampton Bldgs. EC1	B35	Old Paradise St. SE11	A61
New St. EC2	B50	Northampton Rd. EC1	A42	Old Park La. W1	B49
New Street Sq. EC4	B42	Northburgh St. EC1	A43	Old Pye St. SW1	A60
New Union St. EC2	B44	Northdown St. N1	A34	Old Quebec St. W1	B38
New Wharf N1	A34	Northington St. WC1	A41	Old Queen St. SW1	B50
Newburgh St. W1	B40	Northumberland Alley EC3	B45	Old Seacoal La. EC4	B43
Newburn St. SE11	B62	Northumberland Av.	23	Old Sq. WC2	B42
Newbury St. EC1	B43	Northumberland Av. WC2	A51	Old St. EC1	A43
Newcastle Cl. EC4	B43			Oldbury Pl. W1	A39
Newcastle Pl. W2	A37	Northumberland St. WC2	A51	Olivers St. EC2	A44
Newcomen St. SE1	B54	Northwest Pl. N1	A35	Olympia Yd. W2	A46
Newcourt St. NW8	A30	Northwick Clo. NW8	B30	Omega Pl. N1	B34
Newgate St. EC1	B43	Northwick Ter. NW8	B30	Onslow Gdns. SW7	B56
Newington Butts SE11	B61	Norton Folgate E1	A45	Onslow Ms. W. SW7	B57
Newington Causeway SE1	A63	Norwich St. EC4	B42	Onslow Sq. SW7	B57
		Nott Ct. WC2	B41	Onslow St. EC1	A42
Newman Pass. W1	B40	Nottingham Pl. W1	A38	Ontario St. SE1	A63
		Nottingham St. W1	A38	Opal St. SE11	B62
				Orange St. WC2	A50
				Orchard St. W1	B38

87

Orchardson St. NW8 A37
Orde Hall St. WC1 A41
Ordnance Hill NW8 A30
Orient St. SE11 A62
Orme La. W2 A46
Orme Sq. W2 A46
Ormond Ms. WC1 A41
Ormond Yd. SW1 A50
Ormonde Gate SW3 B58
Ormonde Ter. NW8 A31
Orsett St. SE11 B61
Orsett Ter. W2 B36
Osbert St. SW1 B60
Osborn St. E1 B45
Oslo Ct. NW8 A30
Osnaburgh St. NW1 A39
Osnaburgh St. NW1 B32
Osnaburgh Ter. NW1 A39
Ossulston St. NW1 A33
Osten Ms. SW7 A56
Oswin St. SE11 A63
Othello Clo. SE1 B62
Outer Circle NW1 A31
Outer Circle NW1 A32
Outram St. N1 A34
Oval Rd. NW1 A32
Ovington Gdns. SW3 A57
Ovington Ms. SW3 A57
Ovington Sq. SW3 A58
Ovington St. SW3 A58
Owen St. EC1 B35
Owens Row EC1 B35
Oxendon St. SW1 A50
Oxford Cir. **19**
Oxford Cir. W1 B39
Oxford Sq. W2 B37
Oxford St. **18**
Oxford St. W1 B38
Paddington Grn. W2 A37
Paddington St. W1 A38
Page St. SW1 A60
Pakenham St. WC1 B35
Palace Av. W8 A46
Palace Gate W8 A46
Palace St. SW1 A59
Palmer St. SW1 A60
Pancras La. EC4 B44

Pancras Rd. NW1 A33
Panton St. **20**
Panton St. SW1 A50
Panyer Alley EC4 B43
Pardon St. EC1 A43
Paris Gdn. SE1 A52
Park Clo. SW1 B48
Park Cres. W1 A39
Park Crescent Ms. E. A39
W1
Park Crescent Ms. W. A39
W1
Park La. W1 A48
Park La. W1 B49
Park Pl. SW1 B50
Park Rd. NW8 B30
Park Rd. W2 B36
Park Sq. E. NW1 A39
Park Sq. W. NW1 A39
Park Square Ms. NW1 A39
Park St. SE1 A53
Park St. W1 B38
Park Village E. NW1 A32
Park Village W. NW1 A32
Park West Pl. W2 B37
Parker St. WC2 B41
Parkers Row SE1 B55
Parkfield St. N1 A35
Parkway NW1 A32
Parliament Sq. SW1 B51
Parliament St. SW1 B51
Passmore St. SW1 B58
Pastor St. SE11 A63
Paternoster Row EC4 B43
Paternoster Sq. EC4 B43
Paul St. EC2 A44
Paveley St. NW8 B30
Pavilion Rd. SW1 B48
Pavilion St. SW1 A58
Peabody Av. SW1 B59
Peabody Bldgs. SE1 B52
Peabody Bldgs. WC1 A41
Peabody Est. EC1 A43
Peabody Est. SE1 A62
Peacock St. SE17 B63
Pear Tree Clo. SE1 A42
Pear Tree Ct. EC1 A42
Pearman St. SE1 A62
Pedley St. E1 A45
Pelham Cres. SW7 B57
Pelham Ct. SW3 B57

Pelham Pl. SW7 A57
Pelham St. SW7 A57
Pembroke Clo. SW1 B49
Penfold Pl. NW1 A37
Penfold St. NW8 A37
Penrhyn St. NW1 A33
Penrose St. SE17 B63
Penton Gro. N1 A35
Penton Pl. SE17 B63
Penton Ri. WC1 B35
Penton St. N1 A35
Pentonville Rd. N1 B34
Pepys St. EC3 A55
Percy Cir. WC1 B35
Percy Ms. W1 B40
Percy St. W1 B40
Percy St. WC1 B35
Perkins Rents SW1 A60
Perrys Pl. W1 B40
Peter St. W1 B40
Peters Hill EC4 A53
Peters La. EC1 A43
Petersham La. SW7 A56
Petersham Ms. SW7 A56
Petersham Pl. SW7 A56
Peto Pl. NW1 A39
Petticoat La. E1 B45
Petty France SW1 A60
Petyward SW3 B57
Philpot La. EC3 A54
Phipp St. EC2 A44
Phoenix Pl. WC1 A42
Phoenix Rd. NW1 B33
Phoenix St. WC2 B40
Piccadilly **19**
Piccadilly Cir. **19**
Piccadilly Cir. W1 A50
Piccadilly Pl. W1 A50
Piccadilly W1 B49
Pickering Ms. W2 B36
Pickle Herring St. SE1 B55
Pickwick St. SE1 B53
Picton Pl. W1 B39
Pike Gdns. SE1 A53
Pilgrim St. **25**
Pilgrim St. EC4 B43
Pilgrimage St. SE1 B54
Pilton Pl. SE17 B63
Pimlico Rd. SW1 B58
Pindar St. EC2 A44
Pindock Ms. W9 A36
Pine St. EC1 A42

88

Pit Head Ms. W1	B49	Praed Ms. W2	B37	Queen Street Pl. EC4	A53
Plantain Pl. SE1	B54	Praed St. W2	B37	Queen Victoria St. EC4	A53
Platina St. EC2	A44	Pratt Wk. SE11	A61	Queenhithe EC4	A53
Platt St. NW1	A33	Prescot St. E1	A55	Queens Elm Sq. SW3	B57
Playhouse Yd. EC4	B43	Prices St. SE1	B53	Queens Gate Gdns. SW7	A56
Pleasant Row NW1	A32	Prices Yd. N1	A35		
Plender Pl. NW1	A33	Prideaux Pl. WC1	B35	Queens Gate Ms. SW7	B46
Plender St. NW1	A33	Primrose Hill Bridge NW8	A31	Queens Gate Pl. SW7	B46
Plough Pl. EC4	B42	Primrose Hill EC4	B42	Queens Gate Place Ms. SW7	A56
Plough Yd. EC2	A44	Primrose Hill EC2	A44		
Plumtree Ct. EC4	B42	Prince Albert Rd NW8	B30	Queens Gate SW7	B46
Plympton St. NW8	A37	Prince Albert Rd. NW1	A31	Queens Gate Ter. SW7	A56
Pocock St. SE1	B53	Prince Consort Rd. SW7	A56	Queens Gdns. W2	B36
Poets Corner SW1	A61			Queens Grove Studios NW8	A30
Poland St.	**19**	Prince of Wales Ter. W8	B46		
Poland St. W1	B40	Princelet St. E1	A45	Queens Ms. W2	B36
Pollen St. W1	B39	Princes Gardens Ms. SW7	A57	Queens Ter. NW8	A30
Pollitt Dr. NW8	B30			Queens Wk. SW1	B49
Polygon Rd. NW1	B33	Princes Gate Ct. SW7	B47	Queensborough Ter. W2	B36
Pomell Way E1	B45	Princes Gate SW7	B47		
Pond Ho. W3	B57	Princes Gdns. SW7	A57	Queensbury Ms. W. SW7	A56
Pond Pl. SW3	B57	Princes Ms. SW7	A57		
Ponsonby Pl. SW1	B60	Princes St. EC2	B44	Queensbury Pl. SW7	A56
Ponsonby Ter. SW1	B60	Princes St. W1	B39	Queensbury SW7 Way	A57
Pont St. SW1	A58	Princess St. SE1	A63		
Pont Street Ms. SW1	A58	Princeton St. WC1	A41	Queensway W2	B36
Poplar Pl. W2	A46	Printer St. EC4	B42	Quilp St. SE1	B53
Poppins Ct. EC4	B42	Priory Green Est. N1	A34	Radnor Ms. W2	B37
Porchester Gardens Ms. W2	B36	Priory Wk. SW10	B56	Radnor Pl. W2	B37
		Procter St. WC1	B41	Radnor Wk. SW3	B57
Porchester Gdns. W2	B36	Providence Ct. W1	B39	Railway App. SE1	B54
Porchester Ms. W2	B36	Pudding La. EC3	A54	Railway Pl. EC3	A55
Porchester Pl. W2	B37	Pulteney Ter. N1	A35	Railway St. N1	A34
Porchester Rd. W2	B36	Puma Ct. E1	A45	Rainsford St. W2	B37
Porchester Sq. W2	B36	Purchese St. NW1	A33	Ralph St. SE1	A63
Porchester Ter. N. W2	B36	Quaker St. E1	A45	Ralston St. SW3	B58
Porchester Ter. W2	B36	Quality Ct. WC2	B42	Ramillies Pl. W1	B40
Porlock St. SE1	B54	Quebec Ms. W1	B38	**Ramillies St.**	**19**
Porteus Rd. W2	A36	Queen Anne Ms. W1	B39	Ramillies St. W1	B40
Portland Pl. W1	A39	Queen Anne St. W1	B39	Rampayne St. SW1	B60
Portman Clo. W1	B38	Queen Annes Gate SW1	B50	Randall Rd. SE11	B61
Portman Ms. S. W1	B38			Randall Row SE11	B61
Portman Sq. W1	B38	Queen Elizabeth St. SE1	B55	Randolph Cres. W9	A36
Portman St. W1	B38			Randolph Ms. W9	A36
Portpool La. EC1	A42	Queen Sq. WC1	A41	Randolph Rd. W9	A36
Portsmouth St. WC2	B41	Queen Square Pl. WC1	A41	Ranelagh Bri. W2	A36
Portsoken St. E1	A55			Ranelagh St. SW1	B60
Portugal St.	**24**	Queen St. EC4	A53	Ranger St. EC3	A55
Portugal St. WC2	B41	Queen Street Mayfair W1	A49	Ranston St. NW1	A37
Potters Fields SE1	B55			Raphael St. SW7	B48
Poultry EC2	B44			**Rathbone Pl.**	**20**
Powis Pl. WC1	A41				

Rathbone Pl. W1	B40	Robert Ms. NW1	B33	**Russell St.**	**21**
Rathbone St. W1	B40	Robert St. NW1	B32	Russell St. WC2	A51
Ravent Rd. SE11	B61	Robert St. WC2	A51	Russia Row EC2	B43
Ravey St. EC2	A44	Rochester Row SW1	B60	Rutherford St. SW1	A60
Rawlings St. SW3	A58	Rochester St. SW1	A60	Rutland Gate Ms. SW7	B47
Ray St. EC1	A42	Rockingham Est. SE1	B63		
Raymond Bldgs. WC1	A42	Rockingham St. SE1	A63	Rutland Gate SW7	B47
Red Lion Ct. EC4	B42	Rodmarton St. W1	A38	Rutland St. SW7	A57
Red Lion Sq. WC1	A41	Rodmarton St. W1	B38	Rutland Street Ms. SW7	A57
Red Lion St. WC1	A41	Rodney Pl. SE17	B63		
Red Pl. W1	B38	Rodney Rd. SE17	B63	Ryder St. SW1	A50
Redan Pl. W2	B36	Rodney St. N1	A35	Rysbrack St. SW3	A58
Redchurch St. E2	A45	Roger St. WC1	A41		
Redcliffe Gdns. SW10	B56	Roland Gdns. SW10	B56	**Sackville St.**	**19**
Redcliffe Ms. SW10	B56	Roland Gdns. SW10	B56	Sackville St. W1	A50
Redcliffe Rd. SW10	B56	Roland Way SW10	B56	Saffron Hill EC1	A42
Redcliffe Sq. SW10	B56	Rolls Bldgs. EC4	B42	Sail St. SE11	A62
Redcross Pl. SE1	B53	Rolls Pass. EC4	B42	St. Albans Gro. W8	A56
Redcross Way SE1	B53	Romilly St. W1	B40	St. Albans Ms. W2	A37
Redhill St. NW1	B32	Romney St. SW1	A61	St. Albans Pl. N1	A35
Reece Ms. SW7	A57	Rood La. EC3	A54	St. Albans St. SW1	A50
Reedworth St. SE11	B62	Ropemaker St. EC2	A44	St. Alphage Gdns. EC2	B44
Reeves Ms. W1	A48	Roper La. SE1	B55	St. Andrew St. EC4	B42
Regal La. NW1	A32	Rosary Gdns. SW7	B56	St. Andrews Hill EC4	A53
Regency Pl. SW1	A60	Roscoe St. EC1	A43	St. Andrews Pl. NW1	B32
Regency St. SW1	A60	Rose & Crown Yd. SW1	B50	St. Annes Ct. W1	B40
Regent Pl. W1	A50			St. Anns La. SW1	A60
Regent Sq. WC1	B34	Rose Alley SE1	A53	St. Anns St. SW1	A60
Regent St.	**19**	Rose St. WC2	A51	St. Anns Ter. NW8	A30
Regent St. W1	B39	Roseberry Av. EC1	A42	St. Anselms Pl. W1	B39
Remnant St. WC2	B41	Rosemoor St. SW3	B58	St. Barnabas St. SW1	B59
Renfrew Rd. SE11	B62	Rosoman St. EC1	B35	St. Botolph St. EC3	B45
Rennie St. SE1	A52	Rossmore Rd. NW1	A37	**St. Bride St.**	**25**
Reston Pl. SW7	B46	Rotary St. SE1	A63	St. Bride St. EC4	B42
Rex Pl. W1	A49	Rotten Row SW7	B47	St. Chads Pl. WC1	B34
Richard Terrace Ms. SW1	B51	Roupell St. SE1	B52	St. Chads St. WC1	B34
Richards Pl. SW3	A57	Rovington Cu. W2	A36	St. Charlotte St. W1	A40
Richmond Bldgs. W1	B40	Royal Av. SW3	B58	St. Christopher Pl. W1	B39
Richmond Ter. SW1	B51	Royal Exchange Bldgs. EC3	B44	St. Clare St. EC3	B45
Ridgemount Gdns. WC1	A40			St. Clements La. WC2	B42
Ridgemount Pl. EC1	A40	Royal Hospital Rd. SW3	B58	St. Cross St. EC1	A42
Riding House St. W1	B39	Royal Mint St. E1	A55	St. Dunstans Hill EC3	A54
Ring, The W2	A47	Royal Opera Arc. SW1	A50	St. Dunstans La. EC3	A54
Risborough St. SE1	B53	Royal St. SE1	A62	St. Edmunds Clo. NW8	A31
Risinghill St. N1	A35	Rugby St. WC1	A41	St. Edmunds Ter. NW8	A31
Ritchie St. N1	A35	**Rupert St.**	**20**	**St. George St.**	**18**
Riverside Wk. SE1	B51	Rupert St. W1	A50	St. George St. W1	B38
Robert Clo. W9	A36	Rushworth St. SE1	B53	St. George St. W1	B39
Robert Dashwood Way SE17	B63	Russell Ct. SW1	B50	St. Georges Cir. SE1	A62
		Russell Pl. SW1	B60	St. Georges Ct. SW7	A56
		Russell Sq. WC1	A41	St. Georges Dr. SW1	B59
				St. Georges Fields W2	B37

St. Georges Rd. SE1	A62
St. Georges Sq. SW1	B60
St. Georges Square Ms. SW1	B60
St. Giles Cir.	**20**
St. Giles Ct. WC2	B41
St. Giles High St.	**20**
St. Giles High St. WC2	B41
St. Helena Rd. WC1	B35
St. Helens Pl. EC3	B44
St. James Mkt. SW1	A50
St. James Pl. SW1	B50
St. James Row EC1	A42
St. James Sq.	**22**
St. James Sq. SW1	A50
St. James St. SW1	A50
St. James Ter. NW8	A31
St. James Terrace Ms. NW8	A31
St. James Wk. EC1	A42
St. Johns Est. SE1	B55
St. Johns Gate EC1	A43
St. Johns La. EC1	A43
St. Johns Sq. EC1	A43
St. Johns St. EC1	A43
St. Johns Wood Ct. NW8	B30
St. Johns Wood High St. NW8	A30
St. Johns Wood Pk. NW8	A30
St. Johns Wood Rd. NW8	B30
St. Johns Wood Ter. NW8	A30
St. Katherines Way E1	B55
St. Leonards Ter. SW3	B58
St. Lukes St. SW3	B57
St. Margarets Pl. SW1	A60
St. Margarets St. SW1	B51
St. Marks Sq. NW1	A32
St. Marks St. E1	B45
St. Martins La.	**20**
St. Martins Ct. WC2	A51
St. Martins La. WC2	A51
St. Martins le Grand EC1	B43
St. Martins Ms. WC2	A51
St. Martins Pl. WC2	A51
St. Martins St. WC2	A50
St. Mary at Hill EC3	A54
St. Mary Axe EC3	B44
St. Marys Gdns. SE11	B62
St. Marys Mans. W2	A37
St. Marys Ter. W2	A36
St. Marys Wk. SE11	B62
St. Matthew St. SW1	A60
St. Michaels St. W2	B37
St. Olaves Ct. EC2	B44
St. Olaves Est. SE1	B55
St. Oswalds Pl. SE11	B61
St. Oswulf St. SW1	B60
St. Pancras Way NW1	A33
St. Pauls Church Yd. EC4	B43
St. Stephens Clo. NW8	A30
St. Swithins La. EC4	A54
St. Thomas St. SE1	B54
St. Vincent St. W1	B39
Salamanca Pl. SE11	B61
Salamanca St. SE11	B61
Sale Pl. W2	B37
Salem Rd. W2	B36
Salisbury Ct. EC4	B42
Salisbury Pl. W1	A38
Salisbury Sq.	**25**
Salisbury Sq. EC4	B42
Salisbury St. NW8	A37
Samford St. NW8	A37
Sanctuary St. SE1	B53
Sanctuary SW1	B51
Sanctuary, The SW1	A60
Sandcroft St. SE11	B62
Sandell St. SE1	B52
Sandland St. WC1	B41
Sandwich St. WC1	B34
Sandys Row E1	B45
Sans Wk. EC1	A42
Sardinia St. WC2	B41
Saunders St. SE11	B62
Savage Gdns. EC3	A55
Saville Row	**19**
Saville Row W1	A49
Savoy Ct. WC2	A51
Savoy Hill WC2	A51
Savoy Pl. WC2	A51
Savoy St.	**21**
Savoy St. WC2	A51
Sawyer St. SE1	B53
Scala St. W1	A40
Scarborough St. E1	A55
Sclater St. E1	A45
Scoresby St. SE1	B53
Scovell Cres. SE1	A63
Scrutton St. EC2	A44
Seacoal La. EC4	B43
Seaford St. WC1	B34
Seaforth Pl. SW1	A60
Seaton Pl. NW1	B32
Secker St. SE1	B52
Sedding St. SW1	B58
Sedley Pl. W1	B39
Seething La. EC3	A55
Sekforde St. EC1	A43
Sellon Ms. SE11	B61
Selous St. NW1	A33
Selwood Pl. SW7	B57
Selwood Ter. SW7	B57
Semley Pl. SW1	B59
Senior St. W2	A36
Septentine Rd. W2	B47
Serle St.	**24**
Serle St. WC2	B42
Seven Dials	**20**
Seven Dials WC2	B41
Seville St. SW1	B48
Seymour Ms. W1	B38
Seymour Pl. W1	A38
Seymour St. W1	B38
Seymour St. W2	B38
Shad Thames SE1	B55
Shaftesbury Av.	**20**
Shaftesbury Av. W1	A50
Shaftesbury Ct. EC3	B44
Shafto Ms. SW1	A58
Shand St. SE1	B54
Shannon Pl. NW8	A30
Shawfield St. SW3	B57
Sheffield St. WC2	B41
Shelton St.	**21**
Shelton St. WC2	B41
Shepherd Mkt. W1	B49
Shepherd St. W1	B49
Shepherds Pl. W1	A48
Sheraton St. W1	B40
Sherborne La. EC4	A54
Sherlock Ms. W1	A38
Sherwood St. W1	A50
Shoe La.	**25**
Shoe La. EC4	B42
Shoreditch High St. E1	A45
Shorter St. E1	A55
Shorts Gdns.	**21**
Shorts Gdns. WC2	B41

Shouldham St. W1	B38
Shroton St. NW1	A37
Shuttle St. E1	A45
Sicilian Av. WC1	B41
Siddons La. NW1	A38
Sidford Pl. SE1	A62
Sidmouth St. WC1	B34
Silex St. SE1	B53
Silk St. EC2	A44
Silver Pl. W1	B40
Silvester St. SE1	B54
Skin Market Pl. SE1	A53
Skinner St. EC1	B35
Skinners La. EC4	A53
Skipton St. SE1	A63
Slingsby Pl. WC2	B41
Sloane Av. SW3	B57
Sloane Ct. E. SW3	B58
Sloane Ct. W. SW3	B58
Sloane Gdns. SW1	B58
Sloane Sq. SW1	B58
Sloane St. SW1	B48
Sloane Ter. SW1	A58
Smallbrook Ms. W2	B37
Smarts Pl. WC2	B41
Smith Sq. SW1	A61
Smith St. SW3	B58
Smith Ter. SW3	B58
Smithfield St. EC1	B43
Snow Hill EC1	B43
Snowden St. EC2	A44
Snows Fields SE1	B54
Soho Sq.	**20**
Soho St. W1	B40
Soley Ms. W1	B40
Somers Cres. W2	B37
Somers Ms. W2	B37
South Audley St. W1	A49
South Bolton Gdns. SW10	B56
South Cres. WC1	A40
South Eaton Pl. SW1	B48
South End Row W10	A56
South End W8	A56
South La. NW8	B30
South Molton La. W1	B39
South Molton St.	**18**
South Molton St. W1	B39
South Par. SW3	B57
South Pl. EC2	B44
South Sq. WC1	B42
South St. W1	A49
South Tenter St. E1	A55
South Ter. SW7	A57
South Wharf Rd. W2	B37
Southall Pl. SE1	B54
Southampton Bldgs. WC2	B42
Southampton Pl. WC1	B41
Southampton Row WC1	B41
Southampton St.	**21**
Southampton St. WC2	A51
Southern St. N1	A34
Southwark Bridge Rd. SE1	A63
Southwark Grn. SE1	B53
Southwark Way SE1	A53
Southwell Gdns. SW7	A56
Southwick Ms. W2	B37
Southwick Pl. W2	B37
Southwick St. W2	B37
Spa Green Est. EC1	B35
Spanish Pl. W1	B39
Spelman St. E1	A45
Spencer Pl. SW1	A60
Spenser St. SW1	A60
Spital Sq. E1	A45
Spital St. E1	A45
Sprimont Pl. SW3	B58
Spring Gdns. SW1	A50
Spring St. W2	B37
Stable Yd. SW1	B50
Stables Way SE11	B62
Stableyard Rd. SW1	B50
Stacey St. WC2	B41
Stackhouse St. SW3	B48
Stafford Cripps Est. EC1	A43
Stafford Pl. SW1	A59
Stafford St. W1	A49
Stag Pl. SW1	A59
Stainer St. SE1	B54
Staining La. EC2	B43
Stalbridge St. NW1	A37
Stamford St. SE1	B52
Stanford Rd. W8	A56
Stanford St. SW1	B60
Stanhope Bldgs. SE1	B61
Stanhope Gate W1	B49
Stanhope Gdns. SW7	B56
Stanhope Ms. E. SW7	A56
Stanhope Ms. S. SW7	B56
Stanhope Ms. W. SW7	A56
Stanhope Pl. W2	B38
Stanhope Row W1	B49
Stanhope St. NW1	B32
Stanhope Ter. W2	A47
Stanley Pass. NW1	A34
Stanmore Pl. NW1	A31
Staple Inn Bldgs. WC2	B42
Staple Inn WC2	B42
Star St. W2	B37
Star Yd. WC2	B42
Starcross St. NW1	B33
Steedman St. SE17	B63
Stephen St. W1	B40
Stephenson Way NW1	B33
Sterling St. SW7	B47
Sterry St. EC1	B54
Steward St. E1	A45
Stewarts Gro. SW3	B57
Stillington St. SW1	A60
Stockleigh Hall NW8	A31
Stone Bldgs. WC2	B42
Stonecutter St. EC4	B42
Stonefield St. N1	A35
Stones End St. SE1	A63
Stoney La. EC3	B45
Stoney St. SE1	A54
Store St. WC1	A40
Storeys Gate SW1	B50
Stothard Pl. E1	A45
Stourcliffe St. W1	B38
Strand	**21**
Strand La. WC2	A52
Strand WC2	A51
Stratford Pl. W1	B39
Strathearn Pl. W2	B37
Stratton St. W1	A49
Streatham St. WC1	B41
Stroughton Clo. SW11	B61
Strutton Ground SW1	A60
Strype St. E1	B45
Stukeley St. WC2	B41
Sturge St. SE1	B53
Sudrey St. SE1	B53
Suffield Rd. SE17	B63
Suffolk La. EC4	A54
Suffolk Pl. SW1	A50
Suffolk St. SW1	A50
Summers St. EC1	A42
Sumner Bldgs. SE1	B53
Sumner Pl. SW7	B57

Sumner Place Ms. SW7	B57	Tavistock St. WC2	A51	Tinworth Ho. SE11	B61
Sumner St. SE1	B53	Taviton St. WC1	B33	Tinworth St. SE11	B61
Sun Street Pass. EC2	A44	Tedworth Sq. SW3	B58	Titchfield Rd. NW8	A31
Sun Street Pass. EC2	B44	Telegraph St. EC2	B44	Tite St. SW3	B58
Surrey Row SE1	B53	**Temple Av.**	**25**	Tiverton St. SE1	A63
Surrey St.	**24**	Temple Av. EC4	A52	Token House Yd. EC2	B44
Surrey St. WC2	A52	Temple La. EC4	A52	Tolmers Sq. WC1	B33
Sussex Gdns. W2	B37	**Temple Pl.**	**24**	Tolpuddle St. N1	A35
Sussex Ms. W. W2	B37	Temple Pl. WC2	A52	Tonbridge St. WC1	B33
Sussex Ms. W2	B37	Tenison Ct. W1	A50	Tooks Ct. EC4	B42
Sussex Pl. NW1	B31	Tenison Way SE1	B52	Tooley St. SE1	B54
Sussex Pl. W2	B37	Tenniel Ct. W2	B36	Tooley St. SE1	B55
Sussex Sq. W2	B37	Tennis St. SE1	B54	Topaz St. SE11	B62
Sussex St. SW1	B59	Tenter Gro. E1	B45	Topham St. EC1	A42
Sutherland Row SW1	B59	Tenterden St. W1	B39	Torrens St. EC1	A35
Sutherland St. SW1	B59	Terminus Pl. SW1	A59	Torrington Pl. WC1	A40
Sutton Dwellings SW3	B57	Tetbury Pl. N1	A35	Tothill St. SW1	A60
Sutton Row	**20**	Thackeray St. W8	B46	**Tottenham Court Rd.**	**20**
Sutton Row W1	B40	Thanet St. WC1	B34	Tottenham Court Rd. W1	A40
Suttons Way EC1	A44	Thayer St. W1	B39	Tottenham St. W1	A40
Swallow Pl. W1	B39	Theberton St. N1	A35	Toulmin St. SE1	B53
Swallow St. W1	A50	Theed St. SE1	B52	Tower Bridge Northern Approach E1	A55
Swan Ct. SW3	B57	Theobalds Rd. WC1	A41	Tower Hill EC3	A55
Swan La. EC4	A54	Theobalds Rd. WC1	A42	Tower Pl. EC3	A55
Swan St. SE1	B63	Thirleby Rd. SW1	A60	Tower St. WC2	B41
Swanfield St. E2	A45	Thistle Gro. SW10	B56	Townshend Est. NW8	A30
Swinton Pl. WC1	B34	Thomas Doyle St. SE1	A63	Townshend Rd. NW8	A30
Swinton St. WC1	B34	Thomas Moore St. E1	B45	Toynbee St. E1	B45
Sydney Clo. SW7	B57	Thorndike St. SW1	B60	Tracey St. SE11	B62
Sydney Ms. SW7	B57	Thorney St. SW1	A61	**Trafalgar Sq.**	**22**
Sydney Pl. SW7	B57	Thornhaugh St. WC1	A41	Trafalgar Sq. WC2	A51
Sydney St. SW3	B57	Thornton Pl. W1	A38	Transept St. NW1	A37
Symes Ms. NW1	A33	Thorpe St. E1	B45	Treaty St. N1	A34
Symons St. SW1	B58	Thrale St. SE1	B53	Trebeck St. W1	A49
Tabard St. SE1	B54	Thrawl St. E1	B45	Tregunter Rd. SW10	B56
Tabernacle St. EC2	A44	Threadneedle St. EC2	B44	Tresham Cres. NW8	B30
Tachbrook Est. SW1	B60	Three Kings Yd. W1	A49	Treveris St. SE1	B53
Tachbrook Ms. SW1	B60	Three Oak La. SE1	B55	Trevor Pl. SW7	B47
Tachbrook St. SW1	B60	Throgmorton Av. EC2	B44	Trevor Sq. SW7	B48
Talbot Sq. W2	B37	Throgmorton St. EC2	B44	Trevor St. SW7	B48
Talbot Yd. SE1	B54	Thrush St. SE17	B63	Trinity Church Sq. SE1	A63
Tallis St. EC4	A52	Thurloe Clo. SW7	A57	Trinity Sq. EC3	A55
Tanfield Ct. EC4	B42	Thurloe Pl. SW7	A57	Trinity St. SE1	A63
Tankerton St. WC1	B34	Thurloe Place Ms. SW7		Trio Pl. SE1	A63
Tanner St. SE1	B55	Thurloe Sq. SW7	A57	Triton Sq. NW1	B33
Tanswell St. SE1	B52	Thurloe St. SW7	A57	Trump St. EC2	B43
Tarver Rd. SE17	B63	Thurlow Ct. SW3	B57	Trundle St. SE1	B53
Taunton Ms. NW1	A38	Tiber Gdns. N1	A34	Tryon St. SW3	B58
Taunton Pl. NW1	A38	Tichborne Row W2	B37	**Tudor St.**	**25**
Tavistock Pl. WC1	A41	Tilney St. W1	A49		
Tavistock Sq. WC1	A33	Timber St. EC1	A43		

Tudor St. EC4 A52
Tufton St. SW1 A61
Turks Head Yard EC1 A42
Turks Row SW3 B58
Turnmill St. EC1 A42
Turpentine La. SW1 B59
Turquand St. SE17 B63
Turve St. E2 A45
Twyford St. N1 A34
Twyford St. WC2 B41
Tybalds Est. WC1 A41
Tyburn Way W1 B38
Tyers Est. SE1 B54
Tyers Gate SE1 B54
Tyers St. SE11 B61
Tyers Ter. SE11 B61
Tysoe St. EC1 B35

Udall St. SW1 B60
Ufford St. SE1 B52
Union St. SE1 B53
University St. WC1 A40
Upbrook Ms. W2 B36
Upper Belgrave St. A59
SW1
Upper Berkeley St. W1 B38
Upper Brook St. W1 A48
Upper Grosvenor St. A48
W1
Upper Ground SE1 B52
Upper Harley St. NW1 A39
Upper James St. W1 A50
Upper John St. W1 A50
Upper Marsh SE1 A62
Upper Montague St. A38
W1
Upper St. Martins La. A51
WC2
Upper St. N1 A35
Upper Thames St. EC4 A54
Upper Wimpole St. W1 A39
Upper Woburn Pl. WC1 B33

Valentine Pl. SE1 B52
Valentines Row SE1 B52
Vandon Pass. SW1 A60
Vandon St. SW1 A60
Vandy St. EC2 A44
Vane St. SW1 A60
Varndell St. NW1 B32
Vauxhall Bridge Rd. A59
SW1
Vauxhall Gardens Est. B61
SE11

Vauxhall St. SE11 B61
Vauxhall Wk. SE11 B61
Venables St. NW8 B39
Vere St. W1 B39
Vernon Pl. WC1 B41
Vernon Ri. WC1 B35
Vernon Sq. WC1 B35
Verulam St. WC1 A42
Verulam Bldgs. WC1 A42
Viceroy Ct. NW8 A31
Victoria Av. EC2 B45
Victoria Embk. 23
Victoria Embk. SW1 B51
Victoria Embk. WC2 A51
Victoria Rd. W8 A56
Victoria Sq. SW1 A59
Victoria St. SW1 A59
Victory Pl. SE17 B63

Vigo St. 19
Vigo St. W1 A50
Villiers St. 23
Villiers St. WC2 A51
Vincent Sq. SW1 B60
Vincent St. SW1 B60
Vine Hill EC1 A42
Vine La. SE1 B54
Vine St. EC3 B45
Vine Street Bri. EC1 A42
Vine Yd. SE1 B53
Vinery Vill. NW8 B30
Viney Wk. EC1 A42
Vintners Pl. EC4 A53
Virgil St. SE1 A62
Viscount St. EC1 A43
Wadding St. SE17 B63
Waithman St. EC4 B43
Wakefield St. WC1 B34
Walbrook EC4 A54
Walcorde Av. SE17 B63
Walcot Sq. SE11 A62
Walker Ho. NW1 B33
Walkers Ct. W1 B40
Walnut Tree Wk. SE11 A62
Walpole St. SW3 B58
Walton Pl. SW3 A58
Walton St. SW3 A57
Walworth Rd. SE17 B63
Wansey St. SE17 B63
Wardens Grn. SE1 B53
Wardour Ms. W1 B40
Wardour St. 19
Wardour St. W1 A50

Wardour St. W1 B40
Warner St. EC1 A42
Warren St. W1 A39
Warrington Cres. W9 A36
Warwick Av. W9 A36
Warwick Cres. W2 A36
Warwick Ct. WC1 B42
Warwick Est. W2 A36
Warwick House St. A50
SW1
Warwick La. EC4 B43
Warwick Pl. SW1 B59
Warwick Pl. W9 A36
Warwick Row SW1 A59
Warwick Sq. EC4 B43
Warwick Sq. SW1 B59
Warwick Square Ms. B59
SW1
Warwick St. W1 A50
Warwick Way SW1 B59
Warwick Yd. EC1 A43
Wast Halkin St. SW1 A58
Water St. EC4 A52
Watergate EC4 A52
Watergate Wk. WC2 A51
Waterloo Bri. 24
Waterloo Bri. WC2 A51
Waterloo Pl. 22
Waterloo Pl. SW1 A50
Waterloo Rd. SE1 A52
Watling St. EC4 B43
Watts Way SE17 A57
Waverley Pl. NW8 A30
Waverton St. W1 A49
Weaver St. E1 A45
Weavers La. SE1 B55
Webber Row SE1 B52
Webber St. SE1 B52
Weighhouse St. W1 B39
Weirs Pass. NW1 B33
Welbeck St. 18
Welbeck St. W1 B39
Welbeck Way W1 B39
Weller St. SE1 B53
Wellers Cres. NW1 A34
Wellington Arch W1 B49
Wellington Ct. NW8 A30
Wellington Pl. NW8 A30
Wellington Rd. NW8 A30
Wellington Sq. SW3 B58
Wellington St. 21
Wellington St. WC2 A51

Wells Ms. W1	B40	Wharfside EC4	A54	Wilfred St. SW1	A60
Wells Ri. NW8	A31	Wharton St. WC1	B35	Wilkes St.	A45
Wells Sq.	B35	Wheat St. W1	A39	William IV St. WC2	A51
Wells St.	**19**	Wheler St. E1	A45	William Ms. SW1	B48
Wells St. W1	B40	Whetstone Pk. WC2	B41	William Rd. NW1	B32
Welsey Clo. SE17	B63	Whidborne St. WC1	B34	William St. SW1	B48
Wentworth St. E1	B45	Whiskin St. EC1	B35	**William IV St.**	**21**
Werrington St. NW1	A33	Whitby St. E1	A45	Willow Pl. SW1	A60
Wesley St. W1	A39	**Whitcomb St.**	**22**	Willow St. EC2	A44
West Central Pl. WC1	B41	Whitcomb St. WC2	A50	Willy St. WC1	B41
West Eaton Pl. SW1	A58	White Church La. E1	B45	Wilmington Sq. WC1	B35
West Harding St. EC4	B42	White Conduit St. N1	A35	Wilmington St. WC1	B35
West Poultry Av. EC1	B43	White Hart St. SE11	B62	Wilson St. EC2	B44
West Smithfield EC1	B43	White Hart Yd. SE1	B54	Wilton Cres. SW1	B48
West Sq. SE11	A62	White Kennet St. E1	B45	Wilton Ms. SW1	A59
West St.	**20**	White Lion St. N1	A35	Wilton Pl. SW1	B48
West St. EC2	B44	Whitechapel High St.		Wilton Rd. SW1	A59
West St. WC2	B41	E1		Wilton Row SW1	B48
West Tenter St. E1	B45	Whitechapel Rd. E1	B45	Wilton St. SW1	A59
West Warwick Pl.	B59	Whitecross Pl. EC2	A44	Wilton Ter. SW1	B58
SW1		Whitecross St. EC1	A43	Wiltshire Clo. SW3	B58
Westbourne Bri. W2	A36	Whitecross St. S. EC2	A44	Wimpole Ms. W1	A39
Westbourne Cres. W2	B37	Whitefriars St. EC4	B42	**Wimpole St.**	**18**
Westbourne Gdns.	B36	**Whitehall**	**23**	Wimpole St. W1	A39
W2		**Whitehall Ct.**	**23**	Winchester Clo. SE17	B63
Westbourne Grove	B36	Whitehall Ct. SW1	B51	Winchester St. SE1	A54
Ter. W2		Whitehall Gdns. SW1	B51	Winchester St. SW1	B59
Westbourne Ms. W2	B36	**Whitehall Pl.**	**23**	Winchester Wk. SE1	B54
Westbourne Park Ms.	B36	Whitehall Pl. SW1	B51	Wincott St. SE11	B62
W2		Whitehall SW1	B51	**Windmill St.**	**20**
Westbourne St. W2	B37	Whitehaven St.	A37	Windmill St. W1	A50
Westbourne Ter. W2	B36	NW8		Windmill St. W1	B40
Westbourne Terrace	A36	Whiteheads Gro. SW3	B57	Windmill Wk. SE1	B52
Rd. W2		Whitehorse St. W1	B49	Windsor Pl. SW1	A60
Westgate Ter. SW10	B56	Whites Grounds Est.	B54	**Wine Office Ct.**	**25**
Westminster Bridge	B52	SE1		Wine Office Ct. EC4	B42
Rd. SE1		Whites Grounds SE1	B54	Winsland Ms. W2	B37
Westmoreland Bldgs.	B43	Whites Row E1	B45	Winsland St. W2	B37
EC1		Whitfield Pl. W1	A40	Winsley St. W1	B40
Westmoreland Pl. SW1	B59	Whitfield St. W1	A40	Withers Pl. EC1	A43
Westmoreland St. W1	A39	Whitgift St. SE11	B61	Woburn Pl. WC1	A41
Westmoreland Ter.	B59	Whittaker St. SW1	B58	Woburn Sq. WC1	A40
SW1		Whittlesey St. SE1	B52	Woburn Wk. WC1	B33
Weston Ri. WC1	B35	Wickham St. SE11	B61	Wolseley St. SE1	B55
Weston St. SE1	B54	Wicklow St. WC1	B34	Wood St. EC2	B43
Wetherby Gdns. SW5	B56	Wide Gates E1	B45	Woodbridge St. EC1	A42
Wetherby Ms. SW5	B56	Wigmore Pl. W1	B39	Woodfall St. SW3	B58
Wetherby Pl. SW7	B56	**Wigmore St.**	**18**	Woods Ms. W1	A48
Weymouth Ms. W1	A39	Wigmore St. W1	B38	Woodseer St. E1	A45
Weymouth St. W1	A39	Wilbraham Pl. SW1	A58	Woodstock Ms. W1	A39
Wharf Rd. NW1	A34	Wild Ct. WC2	B41	Woodstock St. W1	B39
Wharfdale Rd. N1	A34	Wild St. WC2	B41	Wootton St. SE1	B52

ADDENDUM